The Do

THE DOUGHNUT BOY

MICHAEL R. DENNIS

Mike Dennis

The Doughnut Boy Press

Scappoose, OR

Printed in the United States of America

First Printing, 2018

ISBN 978-1-7323485-0-9

The Doughnut Boy Press

34050 Skyway Dr

Scappoose, OR 97056

www.thedoughnutboy.com

Hippocrates is said to have coined the phrase, "desperate times call for desperate measures." When nothing less than the fate of the world hung in the balance, there were few rules. Fourteen years old, underage, and alone, The Doughnut Boy, whose official records are still locked under a presidential seal, was a perfect candidate for an audacious plan. Obscure his existence behind a blizzard of confusing records while he's trained to mimic his enemy, kill him with bare hands, and become an inconspicuous fly on the wall in the most dangerous place on earth. Before the last act was played out, fate played a trump card, and The Doughnut Boy who knew too much became a liability. Don't believe everything you read in official documents.

"History is written by the victors."

– Winston Churchill

Contents

Part IV. THE RECORDS

Part V. IN THE END...WAS THE BEGINNING

About the Book

The Doughnut Boy, my father, fourteen, was dropped into an adult world as it geared up for another world war. When his father died suddenly, his mother gathered her youngest son, abandoned their home in the Northwest, fled to her family home in Norfolk, Virginia, and left my dad to his own devices. Effectively an orphan, no family ties, he was the ideal candidate for a program that would be hidden from the world for the next seventy-five years. The United States government, unprepared for another world war, desperately needed insight into the mind of its enemies. Who better to train to be a spy than a child, non-threatening, someone who could hide in plain sight?

In 1944, a civilian with no military ties, he lived with the local baker, posed as his displaced refugee nephew, and delivered Hitler's standing order for pastry to the German army headquarters in Berlin. While there, Dad hung out, visited with the officers, then repeated what he'd heard to the baker, an anti-Nazi German spy. When I asked him if he had ever been afraid, he said, "No, I was seventeen, bulletproof, and besides, who doesn't love the doughnut boy?"

For the most part, my father refused to talk about his history, but our family life was constantly interrupted by odd interactions with total strangers when we walked into their bakery, butcher shop, or small store. The proprietor, who looked like death itself had walked in the door when he saw Dad, desperately searched the corners of his own building for an escape hatch. The two of them would immediately fall into an intensely emotional conversation in German after which I peppered Dad with questions about what had just happened. His explanations, obvious lies, nonetheless prodded my curiosity and would eventually result in this book.

In the search for my father, I acquired hundreds of pages of records, most of which would turn out to be a complex fabrication. Because his actual records are locked under presidential seal until 2045, this story can't be a definitive history of his experience. Instead, it's my personal story of the stress of a life lived in the shadows of the most dangerous place on earth, a place where had he been caught, he would have been summarily hung by piano wire, and how that trauma would ripple across time.

The search led to a completely unexpected secret, probably the best-kept secret to come out of World War II. What really happened to the bad guys?

MICHAEL R. DENNIS AND GAYLE CROWDER

Introduction

Welcome to the inside of a mystery, a lifetime search for under-standing of a person most close, central to my life, yet invisible. Everyone has someone like my father in their life, someone you might have been in conflict with, someone who drove you crazy, and without whom your life would have been significantly less or not at all.

Come with us on a journey and discover your own significant others. If I've told my stories well, you'll recall your own. Some will be familiar, some new to you, and others a complete surprise.

New to me, and a pleasant surprise, is my Research Assistant, Gayle Crowder, without whom this story would never have seen the light of day.

Thank you, Gayle.

-Mike Dennis

Research Assistant & Editor

"I'd like to learn more about my father," Mike Dennis, my friend and mentor, said as he plunked down a sheaf of black-and-white photocopied papers on my desk. "Since you like to do research, why don't you see what you can dig up?"

"Sure!" I said, and thought, *this should be fun* as I picked up the first page, a U.S. Army enlistment record for James H. Dennis dated December 1945. *Oh, boy!!*

Little did I know that four years and thousands of hours of research later, this book would be the culmination of our joint effort to unearth the details about this man I never met who passed away when I was three.

The first big roadblock, how to extract information from strangers about a non-family member in this age of privacy regulations, even regarding the deceased, proved a non-issue when I stopped introducing myself as a research assistant and simply said, "I'm trying to learn about my adopted grandfather." People are inclined to open up when you ask about a loved one, and I used the phrase so often and with such persuasion that eventually, even I was convinced. That's a tactic I never shared with Mike during the course of research, but it was very effective, and it turns out, you can get to know someone very well through records, stories, newspaper articles, and other people's memories. It's lots of fun to have an "adopted grandfather" and help tell his story.

Tell it we did, to the historical societies, records analysts, librarians, and everyone else we could think of who might provide information or advice. Everyone listened, intrigued, asked the right questions, and offered to help us with anything we asked. Many of them became friends along the way.

We penned letters to official entities to request information and received documents, rejections, and sometimes complete and utter silence ("Thundering silence," as Dr. Don Pittman would say.) I spent hours on the phone with historians, police departments, museums, and people from a past so far back I could hardly believe they were still alive. When I called James' first church in Haines, Oregon, the pastor put me in touch with a lady who'd been a member of the congregation since James and his family arrived in 1961. She remembered James, Joyce, Mike, and his brothers and sisters, and talked about each with great enthusiasm during our phone call. I thought nothing of it when she asked for my address. A week later, a letter arrived in the mail with an old color picture of the family at the church. That was not the only thoughtful or priceless gift we received.

Western Washington University sent not only his transcript but photos from the yearbook. The National Archives sent O.S.S. records for James H. Dennis free of charge. We received discharge papers, a medal, and a lapel pin that he couldn't get while alive. Many of Mike's friends, some of whom he hadn't seen in thirty years or more, offered anecdotes, memories, and accepted my presence without question. I spent two hours on the phone with Mike's Aunt Jo, and she told me all about Mike's parents and his early childhood. We drove twice to Long Beach, Washington to visit with her, and she shared stories with Mike that he'd never heard. During a few weekend visits to the Pittman farm where Mike lived and worked as a teenager, those salt-of-the-earth folks became family to me, too. Priceless.

The best part of research is sharing what you discover, and I can't even estimate how many late-night and weekend emails and phone calls Mike and I exchanged to share our latest "find". We learned that even the smallest detail, no matter how inconsequential it may seem, is important and can make all the difference. Every nugget encourages you to keep looking, and you find that even when it seems there's nothing left to discover, James H. Dennis isn't quite done with you yet.

"We need a big space to write notes. I think we should write everything on your office wall," Mike suggested on the day we began this journey. "We can always paint over it later." *Write on the wall? How fun is that!* With dry-erase paint, I transformed the wall into a floor-to-ceiling whiteboard, and my office became Command Central. Last fall, I went on vacation and really missed my office wall and my research, so I spent my free time on the Washington coast writing a timeline on giant Post-It pages. Best vacation ever! When I returned to the office, I stuck the Post-Its to, where else, the Wall, and not long after, the book finally came together.

As this circle and the book are closing, Mike and I are contemplating the next. Research about James turned into a genealogy odyssey that spans two thousand years, revealed a history of spies and boatbuilders in his family, and gave me 28 new adopted grandfathers to get to know.

Their names will soon be written on the Wall. I can hardly wait.

-Gayle Crowder

Acknowledgments

Special thanks to my wife, Jude Dennis, who was more than patient with the time-consuming creative process, but also read and reread the manuscript in a search for errors and inconsistencies.

A special thanks to my second family, the Pittmans. For Dr. Don's example of unquenchable curiosity, "I wonder why this fish died? Let's take it to the kitchen and do an autopsy," Mamma Corleen's bottomless affection, and a lifetime of friendship with five borrowed siblings.

Thanks to Chris Crowder for the patience and good humor during all the time Gayle spent working on this book, for your invaluable assistance with graphic design, computer expertise, and for teaching her how to be a sleuth many years ago.

Steve Polimeni, thanks for your recollections and sixty-four years of continuous friendship.

Thanks so much, Jim Dennis, for your story of how the distortions that surround the Doughnut Boy rippled forward in time to impact you and your relationship with the US spymasters.

Judy Driscoll, we found you at the beginning of our research, thank goodness! Thank you for providing the Young family history, for pointing us to the right resource when we asked that silly question about bowling alleys in Poulsbo, and for becoming a friend. Thanks also for your insight after reading this book before it was quite finished.

Thank you, Shirley Widner, for reading and rereading the book as it came together. Your observations and kind words encouraged us to keep moving forward.

Vickey Ritchie, thanks for being our guinea pig, the first person other than Jude to read the book in its early stages. That version hadn't quite been organized, and your suggestions were valuable as the book progressed.

A special thank you to Jo Dennis for your recollections and stories.

Thanks to Pat Dennis for your memories and for helping Aunt Jo.

Special thanks to Nori Muster, Bill Muster's daughter, for your enthusiastic help.

Thanks to my late Grandma Ethel for her letters and stories.

A special thanks to Evelyne Fisher, who remembered our family at Haines and sent us a postcard with the family picture that my mother mailed her in the early 1970s.

Thanks to The Doughnut Boy Himself, likely subject to a secrecy oath, for answering my youthful questions with as much detail as he felt he could.

Prologue

The Prisoner's Tale

We stood in the corner of the exercise yard and watched them coming, the warden, head guard, and the doughy-looking guy in the goofy wool overcoat. Everyone knew why he was here; a local preacher, he'd volunteered to take the place of the chaplain I stabbed last week.

Stupid.

The visitor lengthened his stride and pulled ahead of his escort.

Perfect.

I stepped out of the crowd to meet him in the center of the yard.

The hell with the guard, the preacher needs to be put in his place. This is the State Prison, and I run it.

Several steps in front of the warden and his sidekick, I fingered the homemade knife in my pocket, introduced myself to this idiot and growled, "Go crawl back under the rock you came from. I stabbed the last chaplain, and I'll take care of you, too."

The goofball smiled, extended a hand and said, "It's nice to meet you; my name is Jim." Disarmed by his lack of comprehension, I automatically reached for the outstretched hand, a big mistake, almost my last.

I think about it a lot, and even today, don't know how it happened. In a swirl of dust and overcoat, earth and sky switched, and I lay on my back, choking to death.

The new guy Jim, who I had an instant and profound respect for, calmly kneeled over me, hands at his sides. Shielded from view by the coat, one knee pressed my sternum, the other my throat, and the knife had disappeared from my pocket.

An overwhelming odor of cinnamon chewing gum accompanied his words when face to face, he whispered, "Listen, son, if you fight back, I'll lean forward an inch and crush your larynx. They'll call it justifiable homicide, self-defense."

He grinned and added, "If you ever stab anyone again, there'll be no trial. I'll come up here and kill you myself, and they'll still call it self-defense.

"I'm taking your knife out with me; you don't need any more trouble than you're in already. See ya at the Bible study. Do we understand each other?"

I nodded as well as I could under the circumstances. Jim stood up, once again offered a hand, helped me to my feet, and for the benefit of the warden and the goon who hadn't had time to move, said, "You should be more careful; the footing in this yard is treacherous."

After he'd served his sentence and moved into my old room while Dad found him a job, the former inmate told that story to my brother, Jim Jr.

The Alchemist, Gold from Lead

Walla Walla Union-Bulletin Church Page
By Claude Gray, Church Page Editor August 19, 1966

Testament Transcribed Into Braille at Prison

The New Testament has been transcribed into Braille for use of the blind in one of the major African dialects-hausa-by a group of inmates of the State Penitentiary working in their spare time with Prison Industries, Inc. of which the Rev. James H. Dennis, formerly of Dayton, is director. The master copy of the New Testament has been sent to the mission field where it will be made available to missionaries interested in working with Africans that use the hausa dialect.

Dennis, who has been in the Christian ministry five years, moved to Walla Walla three months ago from Dayton where he had served as minister of the Conservative Baptist Church two years. His earlier ministerial experience was in Haines, Ore.

When he first went to Dayton, Dennis began a Bible class at the penitentiary for inmates. This has grown into Prison Ministries, Inc., one aspect of which is the training of a group of some 20 inmates in the transcribing of Braille for the blind.

Work in Spare Time

Now Dennis is spending two days a week at the Penitentiary, one day weekly during the summer months, training inmates who work in their spare time in the Braille transcribing. The Library of Congress has issued a Braille transcribing manual that is used. After the inmates are certified by the Library of Congress they secure certificates of completion and then are eligible to operate the Braille writing machines of which Prison Industries now has three at the prison.

Bible classes also are conducted. The work of Dennis is done both in the Minimum Security Building and in the main prison.

He left the Dayton pastorate because of a "call" to enter his present field. He depends on contributions from the interested public to support his work. Church groups of the Northwest are contributing to support his activities which are inter-denominational.

Taught Earlier

Before becoming converted Dennis was engaged in speech and hearing remedial work in the Portland district. He secured training in that field at the Western Washington State College, Bellingham.

He is serving as interim pastor of the Bethel Baptist Church in Milton-Freewater now and speaks on call in different churches of the district.

Dennis will spend the next couple of weeks visiting prisons in

California telling about the work in which he is engaged at the local prison.

There are five children in the Dennis family which resides at 828 N. 9th.

Hand-to-Hand Combat

Like much of his life before taking on the role of Dad, my father never said a word about either the prison incident or where he'd learned to do whatever it was he'd done, although there had been a lot of clues.

On the subject of self defense, his words echoed those of ruthless O.S.S. trainer William E. Fairbairn who famously told new recruits, "Forget any idea of gentlemanly conduct or fighting fair."

"I never want to hear that you started a fight but, if you can't avoid a bully, teach him a lesson and send a message to the rest. Forget the stupid notion of a 'fair fight.' Pick up an equalizer, a stick, bottle, or lacking something else, let him hit you so he gets close enough for you to grab his head. Sink your thumbs into his eyes and hang on until he loses enthusiasm for the contest. It won't take long."

Years later, son of the new preacher in town, a perennial target in a school full of bullies, I got pushed into an unwanted confrontation when I couldn't talk my way out of it.

Larry G., three years my elder, a young friend of Dad's and respected by one and all, suggested, "If you don't deal with this now, they'll find you someplace where I can't help keep it a fair fight."

Surrounded by a host of bloodthirsty hangers-on, a practiced ninth-grade pugilist prepared to make short work of me, and I resolved to test the theory.

My assailant, trained in fancy footwork, danced to and fro and made it impossible to get close enough to try out the eye socket squeeze, so I stuck out my head and presented my nose with its weak vessels. He took the bait.

Bash! Unpleasant and painful, my easily bloodied nose let loose with a gusher of blood I purposely blew in his face, a surprise that caused him to hesitate. It would be overstating my prowess to say I took the opportunity to try out Dad's eyeball squeeze when, more accurately, I leaned forward, eyes closed, groped until I connected with his face, and then adrenaline climbed in the driver's seat. We went down in a heap, and it took three kids to pry my hands from his luckless eyeballs. The crowd hissed and booed, "You cheated," but it would be a year and a half before anyone bothered me again.

Fifty-four years later, Larry told me this.

"Your Dad was the most extraordinary preacher who ever came to Dayton. Within the first week, he'd been to every store and shop in town to introduce himself. For two years, before every sports game at the high school, he met with the team in the locker room for a little pep talk and helped out in the bucking chutes at all the rodeos.

"My mother and father decided he had to leave the church when he took to hanging out with the farmers and cowboys having breakfast at the tavern before they went to work.

"Everyone in town loved him. I loved him."

Failure to Yield

His quick, comfortable familiarity didn't end with farmers and cowboys.

A close encounter of the worst kind, I almost ran over a motorcycle cop when I pulled out from a stop sign.

I'd waited for a speeding car that came from the right, pulled out as he went by, continued to watch him then turned to see the cop on my right front fender. Blue tire smoke obscured the view when we both anchored our vehicles. I came to a stop in the middle of the street; the cop dumped the bike.

Sixteen, a new driver, I took time to calm my nerves while I sorted the appropriate paperwork from the mess in the glove box, and the cop's hands shook as he wrote out the ticket. I struggled to read his shaky scrawl.

'Failure to yield right of way.'

What the heck, are you nuts? You came out of an alley to chase that guy who zoomed by.

"Here's your ticket. Call the number on the bottom to arrange a visit with the juvenile judge."

"Okay."

The guy's a mess; there'll be time to work this out with the judge...

"You got a what?" asked Dad.

"Failure to yield. I almost ran over a motorcycle cop when he pulled out of an alley to chase a speeder."

"In the Chevy wagon? That underpowered thing can't get out of its own way."

"I tried to tell him, but he was shaking too hard to talk."

"I know the judge. He's gonna play hardball with you, accuse you of all kinds of crazy things. Don't pay any attention to him, don't argue. Answer his questions, but don't volunteer any-thing..."

"So, you finally stopped one!" exclaimed the judge.

"Excuse me? What does that mean?"

"You got a ticket."

"Yes, Sir."

"Did you run over the cop on purpose?"

"I didn't hit him, Sir."

"You didn't?"

"No, Sir."

"Okay, in that case, don't do it again. Have you learned your les-son?"

What lesson?

"Yes, Sir."

"Don't let it happen again."

"Okay."

"You can go."

"Thank you, Sir."

Thank you, Dad; for what exactly, I'm not sure.

The Last One

With a broken ankle, cast from toes to hip, I hiked through a foot of new snow on my way to the clinic to have the plaster changed. I must have looked like an easy target to another bully when he came around the corner in the opposite direction, immediately bore down on me with a menacing leer, and sneered, "I'm gonna kill you."

What's wrong with this guy?

Far from an easy mark, a trained gymnast with months of practice on the crutches, I was armed to the teeth.

Hasn't he noticed? I've got a five-foot-long club in each hand.

The event ended before it began when the would-be attacker made a complete somersault through the air after I drew back the right crutch and let fly as soon as he got into range. He lay lifeless as crimson stained the snow under his head.

I hobbled around the corner to the grocery store, struggled with the glass door, stumbled inside and announced, "Hey, there's an unconscious kid in the alley. I think he's bleeding."

Three men rushed past me to go to his aid, and a nice lady helped me out the door where I resumed my slippery hike to the clinic. If he lived, the bully wasn't about to tell anyone how he'd been bested by a gimp with a broken ankle.

Thanks, Dad.

Eins, Zwei, Drei

He taught me to count in German before I could do it in English. I still can.

German immigrant strangers introduced by mutual friends were surprised, then pleased when he easily conversed with them in not only their language but also their dialect, High German,

Low German, Dutch, or Swiss. It was a neat trick for a guy who left school before his ninth-grade experience was three weeks old, and so Norwegian his direct family line goes back to and beyond the first king of Norway. No one in our family spoke German or, for that matter, Norwegian.

Other Germans he met by accident when we walked into their grocery store, bakery, or butcher shop were much less pleased to see him. Instant recognition for both; Dad a little surprised, the shopkeeper, wide-eyed, looked as if death itself had walked in the door and searched frantically for an escape route.

Not this again.

I had no idea what they were afraid of but recognized their fear because I'd also had occasion to fear him. Although most days he behaved like a big kid, and a great deal of fun, he could be very scary when, unannounced, something uncorked an artesian well of unregulated anger. At the time, no one had a clue; today it's called post-traumatic stress disorder.

PART I

MIKE

1.

The Amateur

"Where are we in this one?" I asked Mother about a picture of Dad standing chest-deep in a lake where he grinned back at the camera, holding me, one year old. I assumed he was having fun.

"Lake Whatcom."

"Doing what?"

"Picnic."

"Were we playing?"

I don't remember him ever playing with us like that.

"No."

"What's happening?"

Never one to spare the feelings, she answered, "As I took the picture, he said, 'I don't know what to do with this.'"

So much for assumptions.

Like most young fathers, his parenting skills were developed on the fly, an ad hoc education that sometimes cost us both. By the time I was two, he'd learned sweets were a good way to corral me, and for whatever reason, I hadn't yet found a need to speak. On the way home from the store, I sat beside him in the front seat and enjoyed a cherry Tootsie Roll Pop.

The red one.

1. *"I don't know what to do with this," he said to Mom.*

The car turned left, my door opened, and I found myself rolling in the gravel.

Miraculously uninjured, I sat beside the road and assessed my only injury, the sticky candy now coated in dirt and still in my hand. The car skidded to a stop; his door flew open, he rushed around to where I sat and breathlessly demanded, "Are you okay?"

I pointed at the sucker and cried.

What are you talking about, can't you see my candy's ruined?

Relieved to find me uninjured, fright replaced by anger, he snatched the sucker from my hand and threw it over his shoulder.

"Never mind that!"

The sucker tumbled through the air and disappeared into the tall grass alongside the road.

"What's important here is, you're not hurt so we aren't gonna say anything about this to your mother. Got it?"

I nodded.

Why'd you do that? We could'a washed it off.

Weeks later, on the way to Grandma's house, we sped along a road of sharp switchbacks. Long before seatbelts, seats folded flat in the back of the station wagon; I slid back and forth, finally had enough, then spoke my first words. Obviously, I'd been listening.

"Jesus Kwighst, Dad, slow down!"

Direction

I was four when a Divine Message was delivered through my mother that allowed me to 'see' into my future.

"Come here, Mikie, I want to show you something," she said, then folded an ordinary piece of paper into an odd shape. "Watch this."

With a little flick of her hand, magic happened when the previously lifeless paper flew across the basement and crashed into the wall with an audible, fwack!

Oh, my gosh! That woman's a witch!

A good witch. I'd seen The Wizard of Oz.

The message was instantly clear: 'Fly, Mikie!'

Keep it to Yourself

"Mikie! Let's go." When my father said go, I went. In the summer of 1955, only five, I was captive to his will and power and had no idea where we were going until, safe in the privacy of the car, full of childlike enthusiasm, he finally shared his secret.

"We're going to the airport."

"Why?"

"For a flying lesson!"

This sounds interesting.

"What's a flying lesson?"

He grinned, pleased with himself. His gold molar was showing, and if the gold tooth appeared in his smile, he was very happy.

"You'll see," he said, then added, "we can't tell your mother."

Again? I wonder why.

"Okay."

Why not, a secret shared with him when he is so pleased can be fun.

He drove north down the long gentle slope between our home and the giant runways of the Portland Airport.

At Marine Drive, we turned left where the snow-covered cone of Mount Hood was reflected on the slick surface of a river normally crowded with sailboats. Windless, it was a bad day for the boats.

Is this a good day for a flying lesson?

Who knew?

A parallel twin to the highway, we drove beside one of the long black runways until we arrived at a big parking lot. In his excitement, he forgot about me and was halfway across the lot before I wrestled open the Ford's heavy door, climbed down, and slammed it.

For adult legs, it was a short walk to the long, low brick building with a control tower cab on top, but my short legs churned as I ran to catch up at the big glass door. Inside, Dad spoke to a man at the counter while I climbed on a couch to get a better look at pictures of airplanes that hung on the wall. Wow! A room lined with airplane pictures.

I know what my room at home is gonna look like.

The man said, "Son, come with us. Let's go fly." In a single leap, I flew off the couch and followed them through a side door. Outside, I squinted, punched in the face by a wave of heat reflected from an ocean of sun-drenched concrete. Half blind, I stumbled along behind them as the man explained to Dad that we would be flying something called a Cessna 140.

Holy mackerel! That's the most beautiful thing I've ever seen!

I was struck dumb by her flowing lines; she was dressed in stunning platinum silver with a green stripe down her side.

That's nothing like my stick and paper planes.

It was love at first sight.

The man opened the door. There were seats for him and Dad but none for me.

"You can ride in back, Mikie."

Outta my way.

I scrambled over the seats to find a cozy space large enough to stand and walk back and forth and look out either window.

Heaven.

2. Example of a Cessna 140 like the beauty I saw at five years old.

Click clack; the man did something with a knob on the instrument panel; the engine stirred to life with a blopita, blopita, blopita, the propeller disappeared, and the machine rocked on her toes, anxious to be off. Another push on the knob and her voice rose, thrumita, thrumita, thrumita.

At the end of the runway, graceful as a ballerina, she pirouetted around one wheel to line up for takeoff, cleared her throat, and roared an angry snarl.

Beautiful, and fierce, too!

The pavement rushed by, and we didn't fly as much as the earth fell away. I wiggled my toes against the floor for reassurance and watched the world shrink into insignificance. From my windows in back I could see all the way to the edge of the earth.

So, this is flying. I like it!

Legacy

As long as I could remember, I'd been welcome in my Grandpa Ronald Young's basement boat shop on Front Street in Poulsbo, Washington. When I was five and hanging out in the shop anyway, he decided it was time to teach me a boatbuilding skill.

"Come with me, I'll show you how to make the glue for the screw bungs." From a high shelf he took down a big can of something then opened a drawer under his workbench, removed and handed me an old tuna can encrusted with petrified brown rivulets of dry glue. "Here, pour some of the brown powder from the big can into this tuna can then take it to the water spigot by the shop door."

It was tricky pouring the powder from the big can into the tuna can, but what ended up on the counter he deftly scooped up with a thin paint trowel and poured back into the big can.

"Carefully crack the spigot so it just drips, and then add two or three drops of water to the powder. No more."

Neat! I like opening water spigots, although, this drip, drip, drip style lacks the satisfying rush of water I prefer.

From the left pocket of his khaki shirt, Grandpa produced a Popsicle stick coated with dried glue.

Cool, he's the only adult I've ever seen take a Popsicle stick from a shirt pocket.

"Now, use this stick to mix the powder with the water." He demonstrated the technique then added, "Slowly, stir it round and round like this."

Oh man, this just gets better and better!

"Add a little more water, a couple drops at a time, then keep stirring until the lumps are gone and the glue is like thin paste. Not too thick and not too thin."

I nodded.

I'd been around him long enough to know that learning a new skill was about watching, listening, and practicing. Not talking.

There was no formal declaration; Grandpa decided he'd be my mentor, responsible for my practical education and important lessons for living. The schoolhouse was on his back porch steps where we sat together in the balmy, soft twilight of long summer evenings.

The earliest lesson I recall, how to shell raw peas, wasn't difficult, and I was pretty good at it. I pushed my thumb gently on the center of the shell, it split with little effort and the neat row of peas fell into the clear glass bowl Grandma had given us to collect them. Some of the peas never made it to the bowl.

Sweet peas taste good raw.

Apple pie required many large Yellow Delicious apples to be peeled with a sharp knife. Held in his left hand, the apple rotated like magic while he pressed the knife lightly against the skin with his other hand. The green peel came off effortlessly in one continuous piece.

Very neat!

The task was somewhat ahead of my yet-to-be perfected eye-hand coordination. My first apple appeared to have been attacked by an ax murderer. The peeling bowl on my lap had a distressing quantity of apple meat as well as peelings. I timidly handed the sorry result to Grandpa for inspection. With a straight face and a slight downturn at the corners of his mouth, he inspected the pathetic apple then smiled and said, "Good enough, your Grandma is just gonna cut it up into little pieces for a pie, anyway."

He handed me another apple from a bowl full of them. "Here, don't worry; practice, you'll get better. There's plenty more on the tree I planted in the front yard the day your mother was born."

Eighty-eight years after he planted it, it's still there.

The lesson I wouldn't recognize until much later, "Failure and practice, together, are the path to success," would serve me well. I picked up my knife, happily attacked the next apple and admired my new title.

Apple Peeler!

Armed with the Popsicle stick from his pocket and the can of wonderfully sticky brown adhesive chemistry I created, I leaned my shoulder into the big wooden work stool he built and slid it over to the boat so I could climb up and get to the serious task of boatbuilding.

The boat had a planked foredeck that Grandpa fastened with golden bronze screws set into counter-bored holes. He had cut wooden plugs from a scrap of mahogany to fill the holes.

"Take the stick and dribble a bit of glue into the hole, then smear some on the plug like this. Okay, now line up the grain of the plug with the grain of the plank so when we're done it looks pretty." Looks counted in his world. His work looked like sculpture; beautiful, graceful flowing lines and tight joints.

3. Grandpa Ronald and me

From a pocket in his gray coveralls, he produced a small wooden mallet. "Now take this mallet and give the plug a sharp rap to drive it into the hole." I could hardly believe my luck, a neat wooden hammer just my size and he wanted me to use it to hit the plug on purpose!

Cool!

He removed his own larger hammer from a loop on his coveralls and demonstrated the technique. Whack!

When executed properly, some of the brown glue would splash on my coat sleeves. These glue blobs, if I was careful and didn't disturb them, would dry into tiny solid buttons. Later, I'd finger the globs of glue and enjoy their lumpy feel, tactile proof of my worth, another new title to add to my growing list.

Boatbuilder.

Buttons of glue on my sleeves like Grandpa.

The glue buttons upset my mother but not as much as the white paint I got on my new blue jacket when we painted the front porch railing. A ruined jacket was a mortal sin that went very poorly for me but, before Mother could get too upset, Grandpa intervened, smiled, and said, "It's okay, honey, it's my fault; he's learning to be a man. I'll take him down to the store for a new coat."

Nervously, I watched them both; I didn't think that line would work for me, but he got away with it. We got in his black 1949 Ford, an "old" car born the same year as me, then drove to the clothing store where he bought me a new coat.

The new one was nice, but I kinda liked my old coat with the paint on it better because it looked like his.

"Now you have a work coat and a nice one."

He understands the importance of properly badged work clothes.

We weren't done with the plug education. A day later, the glue had dried, and the plugs stood proud of the surface of the planks. It was time to cut down the forest of short tree trunks that protruded from the holes. From yet another coverall pocket, Grandpa produced a razor-sharp steel chisel that had a smooth, translucent yellow plastic handle with a black knob on its end.

"Hold the chisel in your left hand and point it in the same direction as the grain of the plank. Now, place the bevel side of the chisel down flush with the plank, then put the sharp edge against the plug. Hold it very still; take the mallet and firmly hit the knob on the handle." Adding a safety lesson, he admonished, "Don't miss and hit your hand, it'll really hurt!"

Whack!

Cool. This is easy.

Position the chisel, whack! Position the chisel, whack! Position the chisel, whack!

What fun!

After each whack, the excess plug popped up spinning and skittered off into a corner of the shop. The chisel left an almost perfectly smooth surface that only needed light sanding with a piece of fine sandpaper wrapped around a wood block. After sanding, what remained were handsome, parallel brown mahogany planks with rows and rows of neat circles where the holes had been. The entire deck was as smooth as a baby's butt. He ran his fingertips over the finished deck as a final inspection.

"Nice."

Instantly, more than a boatbuilder, I was a *Boatbuilder Artist.*

A distinction no one can take away from me.

More to the training than a shop skill, I also absorbed Grandpa's philosophy, "a good boat and a good man are a joy," family history, and gained an appreciation for people, things, and events which happened in a long ago 'then'.

Much later, in a future 'now,' I became obsessed with replicating one of his boats. It took six years to gather enough information, locate the appropriate materials, and two years to build it.

Eight years in gestation, she needed a name. Mother suggested the perfect one.

Legacy.

4. Legacy at Ram Island in the San Juan Islands, Washington State

The Mini Mechanic

When I was seven, Dad gave me a jeweler's toolkit he'd bought at a junk store and a photographer's light meter from his own camera bag. He looked at me with a funny light in his eyes and said, "Take it apart. See if you can figure out how it works."

Cool.

I did both. Took it apart and figured out how it worked.

Next, he brought home an electric clock. Not one of those sissy battery things with their invisible works in a tiny anonymous plastic case, but a large black wood and glass box, obviously assembled by a person with steady hands, an artist's heart, and a craftsman's eye. It had a fat black cord that plugged into the wall.

I opened the back to find it chock full of beautiful, gleaming brass gears going 'round and 'round and miniature golden screws, everywhere.

Wow!

Same funny light, same message, "Take it apart. Figure out how it works."

I did; took it apart and then put it back together, over and over until I got bored and raised the stakes. To keep things interesting, I did it while plugged in and running.

No one noticed.

At our house life is about lessons. Not applause.

The Demon

The summer before my eighth birthday, our family along with several others had been to the river where we liked to snorkel and chase fish. After the fun, Dad said, "Mike, gather up the gear and put it in the car." I did as he requested but when we arrived home, a borrowed face mask was missing. Frustration, fueled by alcohol, split the atom. There was little point in attempting a negotiation or offering an explanation when he turned on me and demanded I present myself for punishment. Ignorance was no excuse.

I didn't ask how many pieces of equipment I'd been sent to find.

Now, the Demon was loose and would have its moment. As Dad bore down on me, his hand instinctively searched for its tool of choice, his belt.

I saw the problem before he realized he had one, and like a fool, grinned. A flicker of confusion crossed his face when the hand came up empty.

Swim trunks don't have a belt.

Undeterred, anger fueled by my stupid grin, he looked for a suitable substitute and found a wire coat hanger that, in one fluid motion, he snatched up and straightened. The wire in his right hand, with his left he crushed my shoulder, hoisted me into the air, and commenced to administer justice until, for no apparent reason, the beating ended.

His heavy breathing and my sobs echoed in the shocked silence of a crowd of friends who disappeared as fast as The Demon when it dissolved in a cloud of guilty soot.

Confused as me, I feel bad for him, but a little more so for me.

It was easy to be compassionate for his alcohol-fueled Demon because along with it came power.

Unlimited freedom. Adult Child of Alcoholics, the title ascribed to the condition today, had only a single rule to live by, Rule One.

Be home for dinner, not sooner, not in a cop car, and no one would ask where I'd been or what I did.

The Perpetrator

Two fire engines and a police car screamed around our corner, red lights flashing, sirens wailing, and I pedaled like mad to keep up.

At the end of what we thought of as 'our street' was 'The Field.' Several acres of tall grass we used as a playground belched clouds of white smoke, and orange flames had already blackened half of it.

Cool. Grass grows back.

Steam and ash flew everywhere when the firemen sprayed water on the fire and quickly put it out. A man in a uniform began to ask questions to the bystanders and, never comfortable with authority (with some reason), I headed for home...

Knock, knock, knock. From where I sat in the living room, I could see past Dad where the uniformed man stood at our door.

"Good afternoon, Sir. Is your son here?"

He didn't answer, instead turned and asked me, "Do you know anything about this?"

"Nope, honest, I followed the fire engine to the fire."

"We have a witness who says one of the perpetrators is your son."

"Well, if that's true, it's not Mike, so it has to be Jim."

"Can we speak to him?"

"Heck yes! Jimmy! Get out here! There's a man who wants to talk to you!"

Dad grinned.

"I'm pretty sure he's your man, officer, throw the book at him! Get out here, Jim!"

My brother stood around the corner from the front door, unsure what to do.

To the unenlightened, Dad's tone sounded menacing, but the trained ear could hear the laughter. Always Jimmy, never 'Jim,' the wide-eyed five-year-old presented himself for arrest.

The fire inspector is about to gag.

"Jimmy, is what the officer says correct?"

"No."

"No, you weren't there, or no, you didn't set the fire?"

"I was there, but I didn't light the fire because my match didn't work. Kent's did."

You go, bro, throw your buddy Kent under the bus. See what happens when you break Rule One?

Ahead of My Time

Born into a family of modest means meant I'd never be a trust fund baby; heck, for that matter, I never received an allowance, and my enthusiasm for aviation, one of the most cash intensive hobbies there was, bred an early appreciation for commerce.

Long before it was fashionable, I went into the recycling business. Door to door, I scoured the neighborhood with my Red Flyer wagon, a broom, and a trash can.

My pitch, "Hi there. I'm Mike, I'll clean out your utility room for free, haul off the sticky bottles that attract ants and bees, and sweep out the dirt if I can have the bottles."

Everyone had them, the utility room, the ants, bees, bottles, and dirt. Most people, too lazy or fastidious to return the sugar-sticky bottles themselves, took me up on my offer.

When I accumulated a wagon full, I made the trek to the 'Soup Store,' nine blocks along heavily traveled Halsey with no sidewalk, only a gravel verge that made for tough pulling.

Soda bottles could be redeemed for three cents, but the smelly beer bottles that took almost as much space in the wagon were only worth a penny. Already I didn't like the economics or smell of beer. This early opinion would never change.

Strangely, the most interesting bottles in a storeroom, the fancy clear glass ones with the amber residue that smelled worse than a beer bottle, were worth nothing. I'd been contracted to remove everything and reluctantly also carried off these loss leaders and dumped them in the trash can outside the grocery store.

I used the money to buy as many ten-cent gliders as I could afford; the balance, anything less than a dime, bought a handful of black licorice.

I dragged the empty wagon, the gliders, and my brown paper sack of licorice on a shortcut along a narrow trail home through The Field. In the urban sprawl of 1957 Portland, there was no wild game left to make trails, but the Baby Boom crowd, bent on finding a shortcut, spilled over the landscape and left 'kid trails.'

Privacy was difficult to come by at home, but The Field was a perfect place for my early experiments in aircraft design. The location allowed me the luxury to rearrange the glider parts into strange configurations without unwanted questions or opinions, a self-taught education in aerodynamics.

In my remote test site, I seldom encountered other kids. Most of them were preoccupied with the activity of choice for my generation. Television.

Decades later, I discovered the following quote from my father in a Walla Walla Union-Bulletin newspaper article.

"If you want to know who's an alcoholic in your neighborhood, just ask your garbage man. Home trash collections consistently containing exceptional numbers of empty alcoholic beverage containers may be indicative."

He got that right.

2.

A New World

Play

He and I liked many of the same things, airplanes chief among them. We spent long evenings together at our kitchen table where he taught me to use a single-edged razor blade to cut tiny parts from thin printed sheets of balsa wood.

We taped the airplane plans, covered by wax paper, to a drafting board. The cut parts, aligned and glued over the plans were held in place with straight pins. When we were done, Dad placed the board high in a closet overnight to allow the smelly yellow glue to dry.

"Tomorrow we'll glue the finished parts together into an airplane-shaped birdcage that we'll cover with Japanese silk, spritz with water to shrink, then spray on a thin coat of paint."

Sounds like fun.

When it was finished, I lay awake at night mesmerized by the beautiful creature that sat on my dresser and waited to fly; most often, a P-51 Mustang.

Our favorite.

5. Example of a stick-and-paper airplane

Tidal Change

"MIIIIIIIIIIICHAEL!" The two-syllable form of my name with the "i" drawn to infinity.

On warm summer evenings, Dad stood in the open doorway of our home and called me to dinner by shouting into the stillness of our suburban neighborhood.

There was a length of time I could ignore the first summons, but it was prudent to move my play closer to the house because the second time he called, dinner was on the table, and I'd better be within a few seconds of sitting in my chair.

"Michael!" This call was different, a slight edge, wrong time of day, no call to dinner, speech slightly slurred, and a tone that implied no time margin. My eight-year-old ear, tuned to detect the slightest nuance, told me that to ignore this summons would be at my peril. Time to go.

Now!

On the run, I took a shortcut through a hole in our hedge from where I could see him standing by the front door. The gold molar gleamed in the left side of his smile.

Good news, very good news.

He was truly happy, and was a lot of fun when happy. His raised fist held a book. "Look at this, look at this, it's fantastic!"

From somewhere he'd found an original maintenance manual for the North American P-51 Mustang, the legendary fighter aircraft of World War II. He loved that airplane, spoke of it with reverence, and referred to it as the pinnacle of piston-powered airplane design.

I could only imagine what treasures must be in a book that caused him such pleasure. Mother, never a fan of our shared enthusiasm for airplanes, harrumphed and offered, "Looks like it might make a good doorstop."

The Maintenance Manual was a breathtaking piece of art only we could see. Our shared understanding of the power of 'The Book' bound us to that one airplane for life. Any airplane conversation eventually circled back to it, and every other airplane, subjected to this unfair scale of comparison.

He brought home more books with pictures and stories of the development and the designer.

The way we talked about him, you'd think Edgar Schmued was our best friend.

Together, we pored over the pictures, marveled at and memorized the machine's beautifully illustrated systems schematics.

The P-51 Mustang was something we could talk about, something we could share. Safe, it became the icon that held the shared magic of a secret sect, a placeholder of unbridled passion for a congregation of two.

It wouldn't last.

The happy condition persisted until one day, without warning, a strange and powerful wind blew through our home and changed everything. The Book, the other books, our shared passions all disappeared like they never existed.

6. The Book!

Purged, a housecleaning as effective as a scorched earth assault, everything swept away in a storm of incomprehensible enthusiasm for something I was expected to share, yet couldn't touch, see, or understand.

Actually, I didn't want to understand–or participate.

The invisible wind had a name, "Religion", and Dad had found it or, maybe, it had found him.

"Things will be so much better! You wait and see!" he said with a smile that failed to encourage.

What's broken?

Without comprehension or compensation, my "old normal" disappeared into the vacuum of this spinning vortex and swept me into a world where the Demon, no longer controlled by alcohol, might or might not still live.

Reconnoiter

Eight months of seminary training qualified him for a pulpit; a vacant one in eastern Oregon needed a new pastor. He and I were driving across the state so the parishioners there could sample his preaching.

A series of new dams had forced the relocation of the Union Pacific Railroad right-of-way and Highway 30, a slow, twisted piece of two-lane miracle engineering that cut through the impossible Columbia River Gorge. Both were being moved uphill, the highway replaced by a four-lane freeway.

The engineers either drilled through the mountains, routed the freeway around them on winding trestles, or blew them up with dynamite and hauled the debris away with hundreds of pieces of heavy equipment. The colossal project clogged what was left of the already crowded two-lane, 464-mile long, east/west main artery that crossed Oregon.

Miles of the roadway had been reduced to dusty gravel tracks, and car windows rolled down for relief from the summer heat let in a fine white talc of grit.

Massive delays while blasting was in progress made the trip in the heat of summer more ordeal than driving experience.

West of the town of Umatilla we passed a hand-lettered sign, ICE COLD WATERMELON FIVE MILES AHEAD. Dad offered, "Let's stop."

"Okay."

Off the road, in a gravel lot filled with construction machinery, a hand-drawn arrow on a cardboard sign stapled to a stick led us to the flatbed truck heaped with melons, where another sign advertised, 1/4 MELON FIFTY CENTS.

Uh, oh. Even I know a quarter of a melon isn't worth the price of two packs of cigarettes or two gallons of gas.

A man stood there with a quarter melon in one hand and the other extended for payment.

Dad's mouth fell open, about to let the melon peddler know what he thought of his business ethics, then glanced at me, hesitated, glared at the man and gunned the Volkswagen as much as a twenty-four horsepower Volkswagen could be gunned. We roared out of there, melonless, while Dad mumbled something that sounded like, "Ducking highway robbery!"

The New World

In 1961 the sprawling new suburbs of Portland, Oregon, my home for eight years, were bursting at the seams under the stress of the post-war baby boom, and my businessman father was now a preacher moving his surprised family to his first church.

At the far end of fourteen hours of tough driving east on slow, two-lane Highway 30 was a place where time had stopped one hundred years ago. Highway Thirty, Main Street, bisected the town of two hundred and was the only paved street. Hitching posts defined the few parking spaces in the little hamlet of Haines.

Sliced in two by the highway and Union Pacific tracks, the town perched on the broad eastern shoulder of the Elkhorn Mountains was anchored by the railroad depot where a sign declared, "Haines, Elevation, 3,336 Feet." Across the street were the post office and two blocks of shops that faced the mountain and constituted the one-sided commercial center. Out the town's back door was an endless desolation of sagebrush desert.

7. The Depot at Haines, OR

Although we had no television reception at all, or radio reception by day, at night my homemade long wire, high-powered radio in the shed loft could receive San Francisco's KGO with its fifty thousand watts, and Ira Blue's talk show from which I learned of a wider world. Unsure of how Dad felt about radio, I kept it to myself.

For some reason, Dad got a bug up his backside against television. If it wasn't the devil personified by a piece of electronics, it at least watered down life.

"Television is a miraculous device that allows us to watch other people do what we could be doing, if we weren't watching television."

25

Master Mechanic and Storyteller

Our big back yard, the combined parsonage yard and churchyard, was large enough to fly control line model airplanes.

Only, I wasn't flying model airplanes. Surprised by the intense desert heat of summer, sweating, I walked behind a gas-powered reel lawn mower with a grass catcher on the back, and my ankles smarted from the sting of the sharp foxtail seeds that blew into my socks.

Miserable, unhappy with my situation, the heat and stink of exhaust that spewed from the engine added insult to injury.

After each lap, I emptied the grass catcher over the neighbor's fence where their goats enjoyed the bounty and, unpaid, I chafed at my life of indentured servitude.

In a misguided attempt to demonstrate fiscal management, Dad told the church board, "Mike will be happy to cut the grass. No, no he doesn't expect to be paid," for a formerly paid position.

Thanks, Dad.

I followed the self-propelled mower around the yard while my brain wandered.

Hmmmm... the mower powers itself, all I have to do is add throttle and steer. I wonder how much power this thing has?

The thought begged an experiment.

With a pre-teen combination of superior balance, lack of judgment and blind luck, I straddled the idling engine and stood on the mower deck.

Bent at the waist, careful to keep my weight on the mower so the thing didn't tip over backward, I leaned over the handle with my arms extended to maximum reach and gently squeezed the throttle.

The centrifugal clutch engaged, spiral cutting blades whirred inches from my toes, the machine bucked once, and we were off. Backward!

Shazam!

Unable to get myself off the throttle, I pressed the metal grounding strip against the tip of the spark plug with my left foot, and the engine obligingly stopped and restored harmony. Another triumph of dumb luck, the rubber sole of my tennis shoe insulated me from the high voltage kick I should have gotten from the ignition system.

The answer to the experimental question? *Yes!* The machine had adequate power.

With this profound new knowledge, I surveyed our shed full of broken and castoff stuff. In the back was exactly what I needed, my brother's wrecked oversize tricycle, the one Dad had backed the car over.

I towed the mower and carried the trike a block up the street to the open door of Willy's blacksmith shop where, as usual, he was happy to see me, a regular customer with no money, but great ideas. His dark, menacing frown was just an act.

I hope.

"Wacha need, kid?" I didn't believe his greeting to be unwelcome, unkind or harsh, just clipped by the stub of the cigar permanently clamped in his teeth.

I need his help, and it isn't my fault I'm broke.

I'd been anticipating the question and wasn't sure how to explain why ruining a perfectly good mower was a good idea, so to avoid more questions I rushed straight through my plan without taking a breath.

"Well sir, I'd like to cut the front end off of this tricycle, take your big torch there and heat the mower handle here," and pointed at the place the two tubes came together just above the engine. "Bend it over, weld the gooseneck of the tricycle between the mower handles that will become the foot pegs, then weld the tricycle seat to the mower handle where you bent it. Cut the pedals off the tricycle wheel, weld an extension to the neck of the tricycle handles to move them up, remove the throttle from the mower handle then mount it to the tricycle handle and... there! You have it."

"Have what?"

Dang, I used too many words, should have given him a sketch. It's all so clear in my head.

"A riding mower is what!"

His right eyebrow went up and over his head somewhere; he hadn't been taken in by my intentional use of the respectful title, Sir. No one in our little town had seen or heard of a thing called a riding mower. Me, either. I made it up. I was counting on his curiosity to tip the scales of his better judgment and needed his devil side to weigh in on this one. If he bit, we were about to ruin Dad's mower.

His eyebrow returned from wherever it had gone, and I could tell he was picturing the "thing" we were contemplating. The machine... and the potential trouble.

"Your dad know about this?"

Yeah, there it is, the classic question.

Old Dad, that is, younger Dad would have considered it through a little alcoholic haze. "Sure, good idea," is what I think old-young Dad would have said. This new guy? The Preacher who I knew was sitting in his office at the church I could see from there, I wasn't so sure.

In this far, I might as well go all the way.

"Oh–yes–sir. He thinks it's a great idea, and a good use for this 'old' mower."

The only one we have.

Both eyebrows disappeared into his receding hairline; goggly eyes blinked while his face turned a crimson that matched the cherry red glow of his cigar when he sucked air and considered whether to hitch his star to this little fool. I felt like Pinocchio's cousin and hoped it didn't show.

Look at that; he's pulling his beard. I put enough bait in the trap. He's gonna bite. This better work.

Back home, I filed off the rough spots and used a wire brush to dress up the welds, then, from a half-full rattle can I found in the garage, gave the finished project a shot of hospital green paint.

There was nothing left to do except fill the fuel tank, close the choke, and pull the starter cord. The paint could dry while I mowed.

The engine roared to life with a loping, erratic idle that settled into a steady grumble when it warmed enough to open the choke. A single cylinder engine doesn't usually roar, but this one had a rust hole in the muffler.

Adventure waited only for me to step on the handles-turned-foot pegs, saddle up, and be careful not to smear the uncured paint. The throttle mounted on the steering bars borrowed from the tricycle fell easily to my hand. For a moment I sat there and admired the collection of parts I'd rearranged into my brainchild, my very own gasoline-powered riding mower. Actually, my first power anything.

I throttled up, the blades spun, and the new machine surged forward with enthusiasm!

8. Example of a gas-powered riding mower similar to the one I dreamed up

It works!

Had the experiment failed, The Demon would surely have made one of its sudden appearances. Instead, when I demonstrated the radically modified mower, Dad characteristically asked no questions but offered what, for him, amounted to high praise, a single word accompanied by a nod of his head.

"Nice."

My new machine, a calculated risk, an experiment that worked, released me from the indentured servitude that was only a construction of my unhappy mind, and I cheerfully mowed the grass for the next three years.

All this euphoria had a small defect, an engineering oversight that, because of the uniquely level landscape of the yard, proved to be a non-problem. The mower had no brakes. The machine stayed with the parsonage and its flat yard when we left for a new home in another small town.

I wish I had a picture of it, but desperately poor country preacher's families don't take many pictures.

Deep Freeze

July had turned into January and the bone-deep cold of a high-altitude winter had settled over Haines' two hundred inhabitants. Winter's anemic sun disappeared hours before when a gang of unruly gray-black clouds jostled each other as they crowded over the mountains and slid into the valley. The hands of my Timex watch indicated 9:30 p.m., and my twelve-year-old boredom meter was pegged out.

I'd been directed to stay out of the way while Dad and Champ worked, so I sat on an apple box inside the open door of the barn and waited while my insulated boots, coveralls, knit hat, and fat mittens fought a losing battle with the indescribable cold. A woolly fog of warm breath swirled around my head and condensed on my eyebrows, where it froze into abstract ice sculptures.

Champ's unlighted barnyard was spooky, graveyard still. The

overcast obliterated the normally starry sky and filled the night with weightless ink, darkness of a quality so absolute, so exquisite and tangible I could almost touch it.

Night's cohort, a featherweight assailant of microscopic snowflakes that sifted from the blackness, smothered most sound.

They forgot I'm here.

My numbed mind drifted.

Man, it's cold, really cold. If I close my eyes, will they freeze shut?

I'd read Jack London's book, *To Build a Fire*: 'At fifty below, spit will freeze before it hits the ground, and at minus seventy it makes a crackling sound as it freezes in mid-flight.' Inspired by the story, I spit an instant slushy that hit the frozen earthen floor of the barn with a satisfying thud.

Close enough.

Heaven

Earlier that morning, the red sweep hand of the big round glass thermometer outside our back door pointed at thirty-nine degrees below zero. Fahrenheit. The sickly yellow sun burned to little effect in an eye-piercing blue chrome sky while the cold compressed the air to create an optical illusion that made the 9,800' high Elkhorn mountains, miles away, look like they were across the street.

Minus thirty-nine degrees, I can kick the bone-dry snow like sand, and it squeaks when I walk.

The drive out to Champ's had felt less like a ride in a car and more like sailing on an endless sea of ice. Barbed wire fences and their locust wood posts had disappeared under a high tide of winter snow capped by a crystallized crust. Acres of ice diamonds reflected the winter sunlight in a twinkling kaleidoscope of color-shifting, swirling rainbows driven mad by the sun's movement or, maybe, just the car's motion.

9. Haines in winter

A priceless carpet of temporary diamonds, a treasure of brittle liquid safely locked away in cold storage would soon transform the valley into an oasis when spring shouldered winter aside.

Maybe this is heaven.

It looked like it to me. Revelation 21:21, the writer describes Heaven. "The street of the city was pure gold, like transparent glass."

Transparent glass? Diamonds? He didn't say anything about the temperature in Heaven.

Heaven might be cold!

Haines in its remote valley was far from the chaos of the big city where a half inch of hated dirty snow brought traffic to its knees. The unappreciated city snow mixed with traction sand and gravel was a filthy, sloppy, gray mud that couldn't be disposed of fast enough, but this endless ocean of color, an incomprehensible feast for the eyes, threatened to overload my brain.

Dad must think so, too.

He stopped the car and killed the ignition, and we got out to appreciate the view without a windshield between us and the miracle outside. I slid off the seat through the open door, slammed it and was stunned by the roaring quiet when the snow instantly absorbed the crash; silence with the quality of a sepulcher. We stood mesmerized beside the car until a gray Studebaker sedan, stealthy as a submarine, appeared in the distance, its image knife-edge sharp in the frozen air.

Inaudible until it was beside us, the car's muted passage broke the spell when dry snow squeaked under its tires and the chains on the rear wheels thrummed by.

Unimpressed by the Studebaker, the persistent veil of unearthly silence returned like the close of a bank vault, the squeak and thrum swallowed whole by the ocean of crystal fluff.

Back at the Barn

Bored to frozen tears, I sat in Champ's barn freezing my backside off and squinted with both eyes in an attempt to penetrate the charcoal night.

In the barnyard, an otherworldly hole the size of a bus was discernible from the night only because a puddle of weak yellow light spilled from underneath the void. Dad and Champ were out there lying under the old blue school bus Champ gave Dad so he could drive kids to Little Alps, the ski area Champ had built with his own hands and a lot of war surplus equipment. The bus, a questionable but appreciated gift, required constant maintenance.

An occasional cloud of condensed breath betrayed their location in the blackness when it escaped gravity and briefly floated through the pool of light. Muffled by the snow, fragments of their conversation drifted my way.

Champ: "... you're not bothered by my language?"

"No."

Interesting. I pretend that I don't know, but Champ's vocabulary is an easy stand-in for paint remover. Probably why I was told to take up this station in the barn, to protect my ears from the heat.

"... not the words... it's... attitude... tone."

"How so?"

"... once at... church film... projector spit... film on... floor... preacher trying... fix it... yelling... 'Praise the Lord!' Those... words... but... tone said... Damn it to hell!.. same difference."

Crack! A distinctive sound! A wrench slipped off a bolt with a high probability of knuckle damage.

Ouch, makes my knees weak to think about it.

Then, out of the absolute blackness of the night shot an invisible, fiery, snow-melting jet of molten expletive. A flash of eye-searing, ear-burning, four-letter heat expanded from under that bus and across the barnyard with enough vocal energy to sweep aside the muffling effect of the snow like the pressure wave of a nuclear explosion!

My eyes flew open wide in surprise and fractured the icicles on my eyebrows.

Gads!

The shock wave subsided, and silence quickly returned to the barnyard.

"Preacher... you okay?"

The sound of the zipper on the pocket of his insulated coveralls where he kept a hanky told me Dad was fishing it out to mop up the blood. "Yeah. Barked my knuckles is all."

"Where did you learn to do that?"

"In the Merchant Marine.

"Well, I'll be go to hell!"

My sentiments, exactly.

The language was an acquired skill Champ appreciated.

The experience left me with a profound appreciation for the two men lying there in the bitter cold, laughing. I wasn't sure what they found so funny, but permanent smile lines were frozen into my face.

10. Main Street, Haines, OR

11. Me, Jim, and my dog Happy in front of Dad's church, Haines OR, a couple of weeks before Fire and Ice.

3.

Fire and Ice

As ponds go, the Haines pond is large, a two-acre rectangle surrounded on three sides with clumps of willow, a few tall cottonwoods, and flanked by pasture on the east side.

On Saturday, April 14, 1962, opening day of trout season, doped with adrenaline, I ran along the length of the east side as fast as I'd ever run. The drug supercharged muscles, sharpened senses and, paradoxically, brought relative time to a stop although the muted, far-away thump, thump, thump of my boots, splash of soggy snow, cow dung, and mud indicated otherwise.

Except for the angry sound of blood as it rushed through my ears, the world had gone strangely silent. Pellets of spring corn snow stung like a swarm of white bees when they caromed off my face. Adult fishermen, eyes wide in surprise, formed wordless questions as I ran past, and I thought, uncharitably, of one of my own.

Why am I the only one running? Get up and help, you bastards.

Then, in a blink, they were gone.

Fishing was one of Dad's favorite pastimes and, like a pair of apples, Jim and I hadn't fallen far from the tree. I'd been ready for a week. Rods checked, new line installed, best lures packed, a fresh jar of fish eggs for Jim, and for the first time, a fishing license bought at the Haines Dry Goods store for me. State law required anyone twelve and over to have a license. An official acknowledgment of my entry into the adult world, the paper I'd neatly folded was tucked in my shirt pocket ready to proudly present when asked by the state patrolman doing double duty as game warden.

Seven-year-old Jim and I planned to walk the shoulder of Highway Thirty a mile and a half to the Haines Pond, his first fishing expedition with me, and a tremendous responsibility. On our way out the kitchen door, Mother, who never learned to swim, called out, "Make sure no one drowns!"

I suppose, because she knew how to walk, the very real danger of the narrow gravel shoulder on the busiest east/west highway in the state caused her little anxiety.

The day arrived cold and muddy, half a foot of crusty old snow still on the ground, but we barely noticed. Just a few weeks ago it had been twenty below zero and the snow many feet deep. Winter had lost its bite; in two weeks it would at least be dry if not warm.

The pond had been stocked with hatchery trout the day before. I knew this because I'd seen the big green and silver Fisheries Department tank truck come through town. Hatchery fish are dumb. Pond fishing would be easy, unlike the stream fishing in summer that required real skill. Low, clear water and smart native fish could only be taken on a live grasshopper presented from a stooped crouch. The incautious fisherman who let these trout see him would go home empty-handed.

The corollary, hatchery fish, were caught with either of two techniques. For Jim, I chose the first and simplest, perfect for his age: cast a red and white bobber with one or more fish-egg baited hooks and a single lead split shot sinker. Then, sit and wait for a bite.

To improve my odds and avoid the boredom of bait fishing, I preferred to sample various spots around the pond and prowled the perimeter with my nine-foot bamboo fly rod equipped with a spinning reel.

The long pole was perfect for casting a small lure into inaccessible spots. The technique produced an additional benefit, enough body heat to hold the increasing cold at bay when snow clouds threatened and shut out the feeble spring sun.

The bait fishermen had built small fires to warm themselves. Behind them, cows had trampled the pasture into a broken field of muck. Jim would be fine there while I roamed among the cottonwoods and willow.

I entered the woods at the north end to work the open spots around the trees with my long rod and lure. At some point, I realized, from where I stood, I couldn't see him.

I sure hope he isn't causing any trouble. He's a good kid, but his attention span is short.

The thought was still warm when his bloodcurdling scream cut like a knife through the undergrowth, and I pictured the bait and bobber rig hooked into the back of his ear.

It happens.

I abandoned my rod, scrambled through the trees and underbrush, over a fence, and around the end of the pond in a mad dash to resolve the source of his discomfort and, honestly, my embarrassment. I cleared the last of the trees, then burst into the open.

What the heck?

A ball of yellow fire with blue legs trailed black smoke as it ran in the opposite direction.

Oh, no, Jim! Don't run, don't run!

A footrace I had to win; silent and narrow, the slow-motion world I ran through, a false reality, was a function of adrenaline and shock. I didn't just catch up with the fireball; uncontrolled, I smashed into him and, locked together in a fiery embrace, we flew to the soggy earth.

Lifeless and still, he lay under me and sizzled.

Acrid smoke curled around us; the nauseating stink of burned hair, nylon, and flesh permeated the air. The back of his Levi's had burned away, and the synthetic jacket had melted onto his half-naked body, sleeves and a zipper all that remained.

Jim's jacket had burst into flames when he'd backed up to a fire to warm himself, then, instead of drop and roll, he ran.

"We'll take over now," said a pair of arms that lifted me off Jim and dumped me in the mud. I recognized the owner of the arms as one of the men who'd been sitting on the bank when I ran by.

You'll do what? I just saved his life! Where the hell were you when he ran by a minute ago?

An instinct for survival kept the thought from escaping from my mouth.

In the next instant, we were surrounded by a swirling mass of arms, legs, and the incomprehensible babble of a dozen men who levitated Jim into the air and whisked him over the tall wood fence at the south end of the pond into the arms of more men who placed him gently in the warden's patrol car.

"You wait here; go home with your grandpa," someone said to me.

What the hell are you talking about?

Mother's father, my only Grandpa, lived three hundred and fifty miles away.

Red lights flashed, the siren wailed, and the black and white cop car sprayed gravel as it fishtailed out of the parking lot on its way to Baker and the nearest hospital, fifteen miles away.

As if on cue, everyone else leaped into their cars and chased the cop down the highway in a caravan that later, Jim would breathlessly tell me was going one hundred miles per hour.

A metaphorical rapture; like that, I found myself alone in the deserted parking lot.

In spite of the shock and confusion of the last five minutes, I remembered to retrieve my abandoned fly rod before I began the long walk home.

"Make sure no one drowns!"

Mother's eternal admonition flared and spread through my brain like a wildfire. She'd never expressed her opinion on being burned up, but I suspected she wasn't gonna like it.

Four blocks short of the house, in a town six blocks wide, I stopped at the gas station to use their phone and call Mother before someone else did.

Ring, ring, ring...

"Hello."

Mindlessly, I blurted, "Mom, it's Mike, no one drowned. It's Jim, he set himself on fire. The cop took him to Baker, I think. I'll be right home."

The line went dead.

Not good.

Minutes later I arrived at a vacant house, the car gone, everyone gone. Alone again.

Should I be worried for Jim, or my failure to protect him? Probably both.

Epilogue

The local Boy Scout troop hoped to gain notoriety from the event with a story in the Scouting magazine, Boys' Life, and nominated me for the Scouting Honor Medal.

The highest honor in Scouting, the Honor Medal with Crossed Palms recognizes actions that 'involve extreme risk to self.'

Diving headfirst into a human torch would seem to qualify.

My dismal record as a Scout disappointed everyone; no Eagle Scout, a Tenderfoot without a single merit badge. Monday evenings, when everyone thought I was at the scout meeting, instead I was flying control line airplanes at my friend Daryl's house.

A dedicated loner and adventurer, I already knew how to take care of myself in the desert and mountains that surrounded us. The Tenderfoot title offended me, and I despised the regimented group process of Scouting.

The Boy Scouts of America apparently feel the same about me.

Instead of an Honor Medal, they sent a National Certificate of Merit.

The bottom of the award barrel.

"Two recognitions are available for youth members and adult

leaders who perform significant acts of service that don't involve
lifesaving attempts: the Medal of Merit and the National Certificate of Merit."

The day after the presentation ceremony for the National Certificate of Merit, a polite little article with a group picture
appeared in the local paper. The sum total of the crowd that
turned out to witness an award for "performing a significant act
of service that didn't involve a lifesaving attempt" included my
mother, father, two brothers, two sisters, the local Scoutmaster,
Vern, and the area Scoutmaster, Larry.

12. Awards day, the whole crowd.

In the faded, torn clipping, everyone looks grim except me. I grinned, a small triumph over the tyranny of the organization. Satisfied this jiggered recognition would be the first and last official interaction between the Boy Scouts and me, I resigned and redoubled my aviation activity.

They don't publish stories about under-achieving 'Certificate of Merit' winners in Boys' Life.

13. Scoutmaster Vern presenting me with the Certificate of Merit a year after the fire incident. Jim is on the right, healed and healthy.

Only four blocks from my junior high school, Jim lay on his stomach in a hospital bed under a burn tent for a year. Unfortunately, I rode fifteen miles on the school bus and could only visit him after school on days Dad drove to Baker to see him.

A visit to the hospital wasn't entirely altruistic; well-wishers sent Jim money which I talked him out of to buy our (my?) first new model airplane engines.

In spite of the discomfort and boredom, Jim maintained his

normal good cheer and charmed the staff of St. Elizabeth Hospital while Dad won over the nuns.

Anxiously, we all waited to see how extensive his need for skin grafts would be, but he surprised everyone and recovered with only a small scar on his back. Everyone said it was a miracle.

Hero or heel, I was never sure. As usual, no one said a word to me, although Jim and I came to our own conclusion.

Today the fish have little to fear from two old guys who survived many childhood adventures made possible by a parenting style Mother described as "benign neglect" with its simple rule. Rule One, "Be home in time for dinner, not before, not in a cop car, and no one will ask where you've been."

Although a spectacular failure of the Rule, this story is one of our favorites.

14. Our family in Haines. I'm in the plaid shirt.

4.

Get Tough or Die

Steve Polimeni, closer than a brother since we were four-year-old adventurers on separate imaginary expeditions, I met by accident one day while we explored uncharted territory far beyond the radius of our parental permits. Our paths crossed on the shore of an impressive, yet unnamed mud puddle as wide as the unpaved street.

Lost in adventure on what I imagined to be a deserted beach, I discovered I wasn't alone when a pair of mud-spattered Levi's tucked into black rubber boots appeared in front of me. Surprised, I looked up to find myself eye to eye with an alien. Uneasy trespassers in a strange land, we stood there a moment and took the measure of one another. I liked the cut of his raincoat, two buttons open at the top with the hood thrown back in spite of the steady drizzle and what I knew from my own experience must have been his mother's instructions.

"Put your hood up; you'll catch cold."

Rainwater streamed down my own intentionally uncovered head and face as I'd seen it do to my current alter ego, Captain of the African Queen, rough-edged, irreverent Charlie Allnut.

Black hair plastered to the alien's head and dark eyes framed by a swarthy complexion were a sharp contrast to the blond hair, fair skin, and blue eyes of everyone in my Scandinavian family.

OCT · 09

15. Steve and me, ages 11 and 10 in Portland, OR

Hummmm, kinda different-looking.

Likely as far from home as me and equally well-equipped for exploring, his all-business eyes measured me from above a broad grin. Post-toddler social protocol dictated the next move, an exchange of vital information.

"Hi, I'm Mike, what's your name?"

"Steve."

"Where do you live?"

He pointed in the direction that led to my home and answered, "In the brown house on the corner."

I nodded, "Me, too, only across the street and down the right two houses. How old are you?"

"Five."

"Me, too," I lied, four and a half, and suddenly struck by an inferiority complex. "I'm the oldest kid in our family," I added to make up the lost ground.

"So am I."

The Really Great Idea

In July 1962, Steve, thirteen, had come from Portland to Haines for a visit that had been productive. In the first week, we'd thoroughly explored the town, were completely familiar with the abandoned mines in the desert and had flown model airplanes until we grew tired of the activity.

Bored with the things that normally satisfied, the hot flame of budding independence began to insist on a truly defining adventure. Something new, something daring with a hint of danger. The germ of a plan grew in my mind until the 'really great idea' revealed itself in a spasm of clarity.

We need to mount an expedition into the mountains, a long one, by ourselves, without the oversight of adults, self-sufficient not for a day but for a significant length of time. Maybe a week. Yeah, that should do it, and I know just the place.

Dad was making his patented breakfast and in a pretty good mood. With a butcher knife, he sliced mounds of potatoes into little cubes and fried them in lard in a huge cast iron skillet. Scrambled eggs sizzled in two more pans, and a fourth smoked the kitchen with the heavenly aroma of frying bacon.

In the oven were a pair of baking sheets with neat rows of his own invention, strawberry jam cinnamon rolls. He mixed up Bisquick, added extra sugar, rolled it thin, spread on a thick coat of butter, pounds of homemade strawberry jam, raisins, nuts, more sugar, and lots of cinnamon. He rolled the whole thing up and cut slices an inch thick, then placed them on a cookie sheet to bake.

With another thick slab of butter melted over the top, those cinnamon rolls were a real pleasure to eat hot; however, the cookie sheet with the jam that ran out and hardened into super glue was a bugger to clean. Dad never did the dishes. That was a kid job.

He loved feeding us, and we made sure he knew we appreciated his efforts. I was on my second plate when I decided this was as good a time as any to present my plan, a plan that later I'd think of as a 'rite of passage adventure.' At that moment, it was only an idea that needed his blessing and also his help.

"Thaksh for brefast, Dad," I said to his back through a mouthful of fried potatoes.

"Happy to feed you guys!" he answered without turning.

I swallowed the lump of food to clear my mouth for the big speech that I'd decided should begin on an up note.

"Hey! Have I ever got a great idea! Do you remember when we went to Van Patten Lake last year with Frank? That was a lot of fun, wasn't it?"

"Yup, it sure was," he said over his shoulder as he took another tray of rolls from the oven.

Good, first yes, great start!

"Well, I was thinking, maybe Steve and I could hike up there and go fishing."

"How would you get to the trailhead? It's a long drive up the mountain."

"You could drive us up," I said innocently, as I worked my way up to the real "ask."

"What, and have me wait in the car all day for you guys to come back? I'm not interested in hiking up that mountain with you. You remember, don't you, Frank drove us to the upper trailhead in his four-wheel-drive Scout, and the hike from there was tough enough."

Good, good, he didn't say no.

"That's it, see, you could just drop us off on Saturday, then drive home and come get us later."

Silence.

I sat, stared into my scrambled eggs, and waited.

"Come back when?" he asked suspiciously.

Nervous and unsure, I'd lost the thread of the carefully contrived speech I'd planned to talk him into this.

"Ahhhh, yeah, how 'bout the next Saturday?"

More spooky, dead air.

"Who else would be going?" he finally asked.

"Ummmm, just Steve and me...?" Time flowed like cold molasses, the silence broken only by the sound of his spatula as he vigorously stirred the scrambled eggs, scrape, scrape, scrape, scrape..... clunk...... then bang! I jumped when he knocked the residue from the spatula.

Still facing his stove, he sighed a big sigh, inhaled and spoke quietly over his shoulder, "You should take the dog with you, and I wouldn't say anything about this to your mother if I were you. I'll talk to her."

Yahoo!

As easy as that! In an instant, we'd slipped into a new world, a bigger and slightly scary one, but one pregnant with the promise of real adventure! No more imaginary adventure, this would be the real thing.

We shoved our chairs away from the table to run off and plan this epic. There was much to do, but before we got far, Dad called from behind, "Don't forget to clean up these dishes."

Dang, nothing has changed, yet.

"Okay!"

Cleanup, a small price to pay for his cooperation.

Assault Any Challenge

Let's see. Even though it's summer at the house, it's still late winter at the top of the mountain. Two heavy war surplus sleeping bags, extra underwear and wool shirts, two olive drab coats, two .22 rifles, four boxes of bullets. Two fragile bamboo fishing poles in their stout protective aluminum tubes, a box of fishing accessories, two enclosed spinning reels, binoculars, two sheath knives, two pocket knives, and two canteens. An ax, a hatchet, a cast iron frying pan; a spatula, a can-opener, cooking pots, rope (lotsa) rope, a large canvas tarp, a can opener, and a coffee pot. Two plates, two cups, two knife-fork-spoon sets and a box of matches.

Two dozen eggs, five pounds of potatoes, salt, and pepper. Two loaves of homemade bread, one pound of butter, two pounds of cheese. A jar of strawberry jam, a jar of peanut butter, one pound of coffee, one pound of lard; canned fruit, syrup, two pounds of pancake mix, a pound of bacon, and two wood-framed, green canvas Trapper Nelson backpacks.

That should about do it.

We were equipped for an extended expedition, one so well-supplied we should have had pack animals to get to the trailhead.

When we loaded the 1955 Chevy wagon on Friday night for an early morning departure, it looked pretty full. I only forgot one thing. Well, maybe a couple more.

We drove up the mountain to the Little Alps ski area, elevation 6,457' where Dad parked the steaming car about 10:30, just in time for the heat of the day. Unloaded, the supplies made an untidy pile in the dust.

Happy, my red Cocker Spaniel, circled the pile once, looked suspiciously at me, sighed then flopped on a folded canvas and went to sleep.

Dad closed the back doors and the rear loading door, slam, slam, wham, dusted off his hands and looked straight up the face of the nearly vertical ski lift where the trailhead to the lake began. 973 feet between where we stood and the top, and only the beginning of our hike with all the stuff.

"Are you guys sure you have enough supplies for a week?"

"Yes, pretty sure."

"Okay, have fun, be careful and don't accidentally shoot Happy," who perked up at the sound of his name.

Crap! How'd he know we have the guns? I thought I stashed them well enough that he wouldn't see them. Maybe he was just fishing.

"Okay, we'll be careful," I replied, and adroitly avoided the bait.

He gave me a hard look, shook his head, climbed in the car, and glanced over his shoulder where we stood with enough stuff to start an Army Surplus Store. The door slammed, the engine coughed to life, and he called out, "See you here in a week," then waved from the open window as he drove off.

"Bye," we mumbled in unison. Gulp.

The car disappeared into its own dust cloud, the mountain grew higher, the pile of stuff to be shifted to the top, bigger, and I'd never felt smaller or less adequate. Three normally opinionated but strangely mute northern ravens sat in a tree and watched us with curiosity. Happy grumbled in his sleep, dreaming about whatever a dog dreams before he ventures into the unknown in the company of his ignorant owner.

The year before, I'd been there with Frank, two of his boys and Dad, but honestly, I hadn't paid that much attention to how we got to the top because we drove the rough mile around the ski slope in Frank's Scout. We'd parked the capable vehicle and unloaded two days' supplies; supplies that had been packed by someone who knew what he was doing. That load had been split between two adults and three kids. Now two kids who had no idea how to pack prepared to haul a seven-day supply of essentials to the trailhead then another mile and a half to the lake.

Never having learned better, our habit was to assault any challenge head-on. We didn't have enough experience to recognize that some things are best taken on in small bites. I looked at the pile of stuff and calculated how many trips it might take hiking the access road. Several.

Then I looked at the big cable-tow that went straight up the mountain, at my partner of many adventures, and knew he had come to the same conclusion.

"Let's strap on the gear and use the cable to drag ourselves to the top." It looked easy and a lot shorter. "What do you think?"

"Works for me," Steve agreed.

Hours later, halfway up the steep hillside, we looked like two broken-down, khaki-clad store mannequins. Fishing poles, gun barrels, and ax handles stuck out in six directions, and canteens, field glasses, and ropes swung wildly from our necks. Impossible to sit, we clung to the cable to keep from sliding back down the mountain of solid granite covered with crumbles of rotten stone ball bearings. The shortcut took all day.

After the climb, still in possession of all the stuff despite the temptation to abandon some of it, we fell exhausted, but victorious. 'It's all downhill from here,' we told ourselves, but it was only a figure of speech. Actually, we had another mile and a half of uphill travel over a trail that hardly deserved the title.

All's Fair in Love and War

The fishing with Frank at Van Patten Lake the previous year had been fantastic. Frank knew something that most people didn't. He stood by the fire and explained, "Many years ago, my dad was part of a group of friends who decided to stock this lake with a breed of trout called Kamloops. They're big, fat fighters that are great eat'n, and really tough to catch.

"Kamloops live in the deepest part of the lake and are too smart for bait and lures; ya gotta know how ta fish for 'um. It's all in the wrist," he said as he turned the crank of a can opener and grinned, pleased with the little joke.

Frank poured some corn into his hand, looked around to be sure no one watched, then threw it high in the air to land in the lake like a miniature hailstorm, 'plata, plata, plata, plata, plat.' Satisfied with his work, he sat down on a log, took off his crumpled cowboy hat, beat it against his leg to blow out the dust and said, "Now all we gotta do is wait a bit. Them Kamloops love canned corn. After they git used ta eat'n it, we just bait our hooks with it, and they'll suck 'um right up."

He was right, we ate like kings and stored the big, impressively fat fish we didn't eat in a snowdrift that had survived the early summer heat in the shade of a fallen tree.

16. Van Patten Lake

The next day, I watched incredulously when Frank proudly showed our stash of gigantic fish to a pair of anglers who happened by.

Have you lost your mind? Don't show those guys our fish!

The anglers' eyes glowed with anticipation as they looked at the big fish and exchanged a sly, knowing glance before one coyly asked Frank, "Do you mind if I ask what you're using for bait?"

Frank the deacon and Dad the preacher, deadpan, answered in harmony, "Worms."

Oh wow! That's funny!

Frank held up a can of fat night-crawlers he'd brought just for this opportunity.

Meanwhile, Dad sat on a rock with his head down to avert a grin and nodded in silent agreement. They'd just delivered a powerful lesson. 'All's fair in love and war' is a dictum that's true of fishing, too.

Got it.

Fearless Adventurers

At the campsite we threw our stuff down, unpacked, and I made a startling and disappointing discovery. I'd remembered to bring the can opener but had forgotten the canned corn.

Dang!

We wouldn't be eating like the kings I'd imagined and were forced to fish for the tiny cutthroat and rainbow trout, a lot of trouble for the meat they provided. I'd really been looking forward to showing off some of those Kamloops and repeating Frank's cool lie.

"Worms."

We set up camp in the same spot by the deep hole where Frank had shown us how to fool the Kamloops but were free to explore the lake because we could catch the minnow trout just about anywhere.

On Monday, our third day beside the lake at the bottom of the caldera of a dead volcano, the bloodcurdling scream of a woman echoed around the basin. The unnerving sound came from the head of the lake, and because we hadn't seen another person since we got there, were compelled to investigate.

The dog, smarter than both of us, didn't agree. Normally he refused to be left behind, but that day, his hair stood on end, and his whole body shook with nervous fright as he backed deeper into his blanket. Stupid dog.

Oh, well.

Pockets filled with snack food, we abandoned him and struck out to find the source of the unsettling sound.

Steve led the way through the evergreen forest with the same grace and agility he'd used to cruise the unfinished homes in the city, a suburban skill easily adapted to the wilderness.

A thicket of pines filtered sunlight through its canopy and subdued the afternoon's brilliance when a second spine-tingling animal screech fractured the air so close by, no one had to tell us to throw ourselves to the ground.

Face down in the dirt, Happy's behavior didn't seem so stupid.

A few yards ahead, the source of the sound was visible. A female mountain lion carried a cub in her mouth across a log that spanned the creek, where another cub waited.

We weren't as alone in the basin as we'd thought. The lioness and her cubs, upwind, didn't notice us. To ensure she remained ignorant of our proximity, we wiggled away in reverse and when it was safe, jumped up and ran to the camp where we'd left the guns, and the dog continued to shake. Long shadows of evening crept through the forest.

"I think we need to build a fire, a big one," I suggested for lack of a better idea.

"Me, too."

The plan was simple. With hatchet and ax, harvest the smaller dry deadfalls that had been knocked down by an avalanche, and lay on a huge supply of firewood.

Who knows? The big cat might be interested in a pair of tasty teenagers for a late-night snack.

We built a bonfire, then sat with our backs against a tree and fed logs into the fire while we fingered .22 rifles loaded with tiny, inadequate bullets only good for hunting rabbits.

"Man, I wish I had a 12-gauge shotgun with double ought buckshot."

"Me, too," echoed Steve.

Much later, pumped up on coffee and still wide awake, our worst fears came true when a rustling noise slowly approached. Happy, useless as ever, shook harder, whined, and backed in deeper between Steve and me. Meanwhile, whatever was out there continued to get closer.

Finally, I jumped up and yelled, "Hey! Who's out there? Say something, or we're gonna shoot." A deafening silence answered my outburst, then the noise resumed.

That was enough... blam, blam, blam, blam, blam, blam, blam,

blam, we fired blindly into the night in the direction of the sound. Lots more blams then, click. Guns empty, the tinkle of shell cases that fell on the rock still rang in a night filled with the odor of burned gunpowder.

When adrenaline pulls the trigger, it pulls it over and over and the gun fires until the supply of bullets is exhausted.

Silence.

Since we lacked something else I forgot, flashlights, we had to wait until daylight to discover we'd dispatched an unlucky porcupine who had wandered into the wrong camp.

By Wednesday, confidence in our ability to survive in this wilderness was at its zenith. Bored with fishing for the big fish we were never going to catch and having explored the circumference of the lake three times, we needed something new to do.

The hike in with our oversized backpacks and all the junk strapped around our necks had been awkward, even dangerous as we clambered over big trees that lay across the trail. There had to be a better way.

We gave it some thought and devised a plan for a slick way to pack all the stuff back out; we'd build a litter to carry it like a wounded comrade.

We imagined constructing the litter would be fun and assumed carrying it would be, too. The former was, but the latter, not so much.

Using the hatchet, I whacked away at the smallest deadfalls and cut two long and two short 2" diameter poles. Steve peeled the bark; I notched the poles where they crossed and lashed the joints with rope to make a frame six feet long and two feet wide.

We threaded rope through the grommet holes in the big canvas, lashed it to one of the long poles, then wrapped it tightly around the frame to make a firm surface.

To be sure everything fit, we practiced loading the litter, stacked on our stuff and used the extra canvas to cover and secure the load. Nice, all shipshape and merit badge neat, we felt pretty clever.

Since Dad had agreed to pick us up at the bottom of the trail at ten o'clock on Saturday, we planned to make Friday a day of leisure, then pack up to be ready for an easy hike out early Saturday.

That was the plan, but the "really great idea" wasn't quite done with our education.

Sunrise Friday, before we could get up to build a fire and make breakfast, we were awakened by a strange soprano hummmmmmm that filled the forest. The morning mist over the lake burned away to reveal a black swirling fog at the far end, rolling over itself in waves that grew as it headed toward us.

The tip of the cloud descended on our camp like a malicious tentacle of smoke. Yikes! No metaphor, it was the Death Angel's cousin, billions of bloodsucking mosquitoes.

We leaped up and broke camp in record time, all thoughts of a leisurely departure swept away by the swirling, humming monster that threatened to consume us. We heaped our stuff on the litter, cinched and tied off the ropes, hoisted the ungainly thing and ran! Mosquito repellent, something else I'd forgotten.

We'd practiced carrying it but not running with it; chased by the horde of insects, we tripped over rocky, uneven ground, then pushed, shoved, and cursed the thing over the tree trunks that blocked our way. At the upper trailhead, having outrun the mosquitoes, exhausted from a combination of exertion and altitude, we dropped the hated device and collapsed.

Breath recovered, we picked up our burden but only carried it another hundred yards before we reached the top of the ski run called "Cow Face."

An incredibly acute angle, the face, broken by two intermediate flat steps equally spaced between where we were and where we wanted to be, looked more like a cliff than a slope. At the bottom, our objective, the lodge at Little Alps appeared tantalizingly close.

17. The Lodge at Little Alps present day

I turned away from the unpleasant aspect of carrying our load of stuff another mile to assess the risk of taking a more direct route down the slope where the lodge beckoned.

"What do you think?"

"I think we can slide it to the bottom, is what I think."

"Me, too," I agreed, "it beats carrying the miserable thing down that road another mile. Let's ease it over the side and let gravity help overcome the friction of the dirt."

It would have been a good plan had the hillside been dirt or a little less steep.

It's neither.

The earth hadn't changed, still solid granite with a layer of rotten, crumbly gravel ball bearings just like we'd encountered on the way up, a fact we conveniently chose to ignore. Blinded by the temptation of the easy path to the lodge, inexperience, fatigue, and wishful thinking were about to trump common sense.

As if loading a cannon, we cautiously slid our load of stuff to the incline and eased its center of gravity over the edge. Compelled by the most potent force in the universe, our creation began an un-commanded and uncontrolled trip to the bottom. When it took off, we instinctively leaped on.

The immediate increase in speed had an inverse effect on time as the disaster unfolded in slow motion when our flying carpet zipped over the first flat like a rocket.

The wind roared and ripped at my shirt that flapped noisily like a flag; pots and pans clanked and banged around loose in the canvas.

We landed hard with a thump and, impossibly, our velocity increased when we raced down the slope of the second face. Underneath us, the load of equipment shifted when the impromptu vehicle began to disintegrate. Never really well-fastened due to the abrupt departure from the lake, the lashings that held the canvas began to unravel, and it hit the last flat with a sharp thud. No one had to tell us to abandon ship.

Together we slid to a painful, abraded stop while the litter, free of our extra weight, sailed majestically into space.

The untidy mess tumbled end over end then returned to earth; pots, pans, rifles, fish poles, axes, and a hundred other pieces of gear slid along in a little avalanche of dust and debris.

Apparently the funniest thing we'd ever seen, we lay there bleeding and laughed like the two fools we were.

Happy coolly watched the whole charade from the top of the hill and, smarter than both of us, turned away from the treacherous cliff and trotted easily down the service road to the lodge. He waited for us with his stupid dog grin while we gathered up the stuff and half-walked, half-slid to the bottom.

Out of groceries, we spent a long, cold night without a fire camped under an equipment lean-to. Precisely as planned, Dad arrived at ten, and we loaded our jumble of equipment in the back of the station wagon. Happy called 'shotgun' and helped himself to the front seat, so we climbed in the back.

18. Steve and me, fearless explorers.

On the drive down the mountain Dad casually asked, "So how'd everything go?"

"Fine."

"Really? Catch any fish?"

"Yup."

"Any big ones?"

"No."

"Anything happen you want to talk about?"

"No, not really."

I could see him in the rearview mirror; his eyes told me he knew there was more, but he never asked.

"You guys hungry? I've got breakfast ready down at the house."

Some stranger I didn't recognize as myself respectfully answered, "Yes, sir, that would be real nice. We'll do the dishes."

I turned to watch the mountain disappear and had the odd feeling we'd left something important at the lake. Unsure what, it would be decades before I figured it out.

We'd left two of my favorite people in all the world up there.

Dad dropped off a pair of grubs and a week later, two moths, escaped from the confinement of their chrysalises, came off the mountain, ready to fly away forever.

19. In front of the lodge at Little Alps, age 13.

5.

Dodge the Demon

I don't think we left the Demon behind; maybe he's only gone into hiding, like me.

Mindful of the possibility, in an attempt to prevent an appearance, I allowed the "new normal" of religious life to draw me into its sucking maw of judgment and guilt.

Allowed?

A petty conceit I granted myself while I grasped for a fragment of my old power. I had about as much choice as an insect sucked down a jet intake and was right to be concerned.

The Demon lived.

In the beginning, Dad picked out the model airplane kit; we assembled it. He flew it and wrecked it. Later, together we decided what to build, I built it; he wrecked it, too. This went on and on until, eight years old, desperate to break the cycle, I borrowed his mower and hired myself out to satisfy the endless suburban need to harvest a crop no one would eat. My plan failed when I bought my own kits, built them, and he still wrecked them.

Finally, age twelve, preteen anarchy coupled with financial independence meant I decided what kit to buy and assemble, conveniently forget to tell him it was ready and flew it myself. The subterfuge wasn't a good idea.

Armed and dangerous, religion or not, new preacher or not,

angered by my plan to exclude him from the fun, the Demon reemerged when my oldest sister, who seemed to know precisely where to insert the needle, sensed an opportunity and told him a lie. I never knew what she said but decided to punish him for the unfair beating I saw coming.

The belt materialized in his hand like a sword drawn from a scabbard and arced toward me. Shock briefly replaced anger when, out of character, I dodged the first blow, then rage took over.

A reasonable beating, whatever that is, became unreasonable when, for the first time, I refused to stand still or cry from a blow. We danced around the room until he suddenly stopped, glared at me, and walked away.

Like that, I'd won, or so I thought. It was the last beating, and the worst idea I'd had to date. He replaced corporal punishment with verbal public humiliation, a tactic for which I had less sympathy.

Our common interest in airplanes survived the Demon's occasional appearance and, over time, larger airplanes with noisy fuel-burning engines replaced the free flight models with their rubber-band motors. These new planes flew in a circle, the pilot at the center, where he directed the flight with a handle attached to the aircraft by a pair of long control lines. Larger planes, longer lines, bigger engines, and increased speed only led to more spectacular crashes.

Wrapped Up

"Where are you guys going?"

Dang, where'd he come from?

"We're going to the park to fly the Nobler, Dad."

"Hold on, I'll drive you."

Yikes, our worst nightmare...

It began innocently enough. Rather than just fly it around in circles, Jim and I set out to develop a twist to the tried and true.

There must be a way we can spice up control line flying.

Eventually, it came: mimic the most historically common application of air power, drop bombs. Not real bombs, of course, just a little model bomb.

We put knife to balsa wood and carved a reasonable facsimile, then designed and built a reliable release shackle operated by a third control line with a trigger installed on the flight control handle. The Nobler would be the test bed.

Having built the bomb first, we had time to imagine the little thing bouncing when it hit the ground.

Does that feel like spice?

No, and it didn't take much imagination to figure out how to, ah, add spice. Explosives always jazzed things up. We carefully sliced apart illicit firecrackers with a razor blade and packed the powder in a hollow drilled into the body of the bomb. A plunger with a cap on the end would strike a nail head and provide the spice.

Presto, low-yield explosive device.

A financial problem lingered. The project absorbed our meager budget and there were no funds left to purchase a twenty-dollar set of steel control lines for the bomb release.

Time to improvise.

There would be little load on the line, just enough force to pull the release pin on the bomb shackle. Although it had more stretch than a steel line, a length of twenty-pound monofilament fish line oughta work fine.

Jim and I sat in back on the way to the park and quietly talked about it; Dad would want to fly first. We'd have to explain the extra stuff and risk an upset.

At the park we explained the bomb drop concept and surprise, surprise, he thought it sounded like a good idea. It was also no surprise when he suggested, "Well, that's pretty slick; how 'bout I give it a try first?"

He had us over a barrel.

"Okay."

"You didn't tell him it explodes."

"You worry too much, Jim. I thought I'd wait and see if it works. It might not."

The plan called for a nice smooth flight, none of Dad's fancy aerobatics. Just fly a few laps, climb up, release the bomb and enjoy the 'spice.'

It became apparent our test pilot had other ideas when the plane swooped high up and over in a wingover, pulled out upside down, continued in the opposite direction then swooped up, reversed and came down right side up.

What's he doing?

We tore our attention from the plane and its lethal load and looked at the pilot.

Holy crackers, I think he's having a heart attack!

The reason for the erratic flight path was apparent as he staggered 'round and 'round until he couldn't stand any longer and fell over like a tree.

The airplane arced up and over in one last graceful wingover and impacted the ground vertically. Still attached to the plane, the bomb failed to detonate, but the big parts of the structure went straight up in a shower of balsa wood and silk, maybe the most spectacular crash of all time.

When the dust settled, we finally thought to check out the condition of the pilot, who was still thrashing around on the ground, and ran out to see why. We found him trussed up like a Christmas turkey; the fishing line had come loose from the plane, drifted down, and wrapped itself tightly around his ankles.

Jim and I laughed until we collapsed.

"What's wrong with you bastards? Get a god-damned knife and cut me out of this before I lose my feet!"

One quick swipe with a pocket knife and he was free from the line, mobile, and possibly dangerous.

If the Demon is going to appear, now is the time.

He looked up from where he sat massaging his ankles, grinned and asked, "That bomb was supposed to explode, wasn't it?"

No point in trying to avoid it.

"Yes."

"Cool."

The three of us sat in the grass and laughed, then picked up the pieces and went home where Mother asked, "You boys have a good time?"

She appeared confused when we showed her the smashed plane and laughed.

"Yes, ma'am."

Nerves

One hundred feet outside second base where Dad stood ready to fly, I knelt on the hard-packed earth of the ball field and started the engine of the green-and-cream Supermarine Spitfire with its five-foot span, tuned the engine for maximum power and released it to roll away in an anxious cloud of dust.

Dad flew the beautiful airplane quite well at first, but each successful aerobatic maneuver tempted him to reach a little farther.

My role as pit crew complete, I sat in the dugout with my fourteen-year-old guts in a twist and waited for the inevitable crash. Years of exposure to the unrelenting tension of multiple roles, adult child responsible for the care of siblings, hyper-alert designated fixer of everything, and crash crew, eventually produced a case of nervous colitis so violent it put me in the hospital where a wise doctor told me, "Listen, son, you aren't responsible for everyone at home and can't fix them. Quit and take care of yourself, or this is gonna get worse."

Makes sense. I wonder how?

Shortly thereafter, the answer presented itself when Dad came home with a job offer for me. "How would you like to work on a small farm; I have a friend who needs a teenage boy."

You do?

It wasn't a question; he expected me to do it and I knew it. Up to this point, all his job opportunities had been 'pro bono,' nonrevenue. This one was a paying job and turned out to be a perfect solution.

Too far away to walk, an extra bedroom at the farm, and too young to drive, I moved in and never really moved back.

After I had a car, I continued to stay on the farm. Weekends, when my employer thought I went home and my parents thought I was at the farm, I drove into the mountains and went fishing.

I ran away from home and no one noticed, not my folks and not my employer, the wise doctor.

My freedom cost me a piece of childhood I didn't notice. You don't miss what you never had.

20. Me with the Nobler, the Spitfire, and others, age 16 in Dayton, WA.

6.

The Curve of Time

My dear friend Muriel Wylie Blanchet left the world while I was still young. I knew her through her beautiful book *The Curve of Time* in which she wrote, and I paraphrase, "Life is less a straight line, rather a curve on which we stand. Able, alternately, to view the future or the past."

Agreed, but my experience suggests the radius is small; ends loop toward one another and eventually close. A series of circles endlessly loop and close with a quiet 'click' and together form the chain of life; strong, yet flexible. We, their children and me, had just celebrated Don and Corky Pittman's sixty-fourth anniversary. We drove from Dayton to Walla Walla for a Chinese Dinner at The Modern Café and unintentionally closed another circle.

My first visit to The Modern Café was to celebrate my own parents' fifteenth anniversary. I was fourteen. We lived in Dayton and drove the thirty miles through the same golden rolling wheat fields where handfuls of bright, white dumpling clouds floated in a cobalt sky.

This celebration forty-nine years later required a similar exodus. Fine dining was still reluctant to call Dayton home.

Time hesitated. I'd buried my beautiful mother the week before, and the pain dimmed when I stepped back in time to enjoy the pleasure of sharing, again, the kindness of these people I silently adopted when I skillfully left home at fourteen.

Farmhand, fence builder, and kid wrangler for a herd of five until, inevitably deflected along the curve of time, my life rolled over the hill, out of sight until that visit. Click.

For a moment, I was back.

Day dissolved into sulky shades of twilight as the sun sank into the Walla Walla Valley while I perched on an old church pew on Don's porch and soaked in the peculiar end of day atmosphere.

Soft evening light reflected yellow, pink and white off a bank of high cloud, and the sun's lower edge pushed a wedge of orange cream light under a low cloud. Rose-tinted, sepia brown and yellow, the valley was a moody, turn-of-the-century watercolor. The turn before last.

A string of domestic white ducklings followed their mother across the pasture to the pond and walked with as much dignity as their duck waddle would allow. Wings beat frantically as a brace of wild ducks in perfect formation silently sliced the air along the boundary of twilight and night then disappeared.

In the distant pasture, Black Angus cows were indistinct lumps and southwest, a sullen, inky black sky threatened rain... maybe not. Still August, the puffed-up brooding sky full of false menace and bravado might drift harmlessly past.

The electric fence charger in the barn broke the stillness and tapped out time with a metronomic cadence, once a second, clack... clack... clack. A chorus of crickets filled the creeping darkness with alto chirps, and baritone frogs in the cattails harmonized. A surprise cool breeze fractured the evening's warm stillness. *Oh!... Listen.* The delicate pop, crackle of halfhearted raindrops on dry leaves threatened real rain.

That place where my incomplete fourteen-year-old self is made visible still haunts me. Grape arbors I built in 1964, still there; a picnic table I copied from a Park Service table, still there; trees the size of my thumb when I planted them are twice my arms around.

Fences I built, much worse for wear, have suffered the strain of five decades of cows stretching over them to reach tender green lawn.

Children on the curve of time are gone. So far gone, they're grandparents, yet still there in memory. Some, in fact, are back; two have built homes there and closed another loop. The others visit often and remain friends. Family.

I was older than I felt, and Don was still twenty years my senior. Fifty years since our orbits intersected when I thought I was old enough, pretty smart, and knew he was really old. Now both of us felt young but moved like old men.

Time is strangely facile. Sometimes it moves at the speed of light, sometimes stands still, and occasionally, for a moment, retreats. The loops close and the chain extends.

Don and Corky's youngest, Keith, and his wife Bunny had just returned from a wedding. From the same table where I sat half a century ago, happy laughter and pleasant conversation drifted to me as I watched the magnificent day slide helplessly into night. I bubbled with shameless appreciation for the opportunity to revisit that peaceful, loving place. My first time there I felt complete acceptance, and nothing had changed. Home again, another golden circle in time. One foot in the past, one in the future. Both in the present.

"Click..."

21. The Pittman Farm

7.

Guilt by Association

Despite archeological evidence that suggested native people had occupied the area for the last ten thousand years, Walla Walla was a city proud of its place in modern Northwest history. It began as Fort Nez Perce, a fur trading post established in 1818 and a major stopping point for immigrants moving to the Oregon Country.

The city experienced rapid growth as a result of a gold rush in Idaho, and in 1862 became the first incorporated city in Washington.

By 1967, Walla Walla, Washington was caught in a back eddy in time. How far back? Forty-five years in the future, the souvenir stores would sell the tourists T-shirts with the epithet, "Welcome to Walla Walla, please turn your watch back 100 years."

My junior year in yet another new school, the Ford Mustang was two years old, phones had rotary dials, long-distance calls were an expensive luxury, electronic calculators didn't exist, and the high school maintained a strict dress code. Girls wore a blouse and skirt with dress shoes. Guys, a button-up shirt, slacks, and loafers or dress shoes. Tennis shoes and T-shirts were appropriate only for physical education class.

Perfect, the uniformity made me invisible. A series of public schools as the new preacher's kid had taught me to prefer a low profile.

Not so for my zoology lab partner and new friend, Eric L. Tall and skinny, he had red hair, freckles, and an infectious toothy grin. Behind the Howdy Doody appearance hid a towering intellect, lightning-fast wit, and wicked sense of humor. He was as low profile as a fireworks show.

Eric felt compelled to challenge the status quo with a visible statement of nonconformity. "High-water" pants with cuffs above the ankle that revealed one's socks were the fashion. I preferred black socks for school and dress and white ones for adventuring, a conservative habit I'd maintain, more or less, for the rest of my life.

Not Eric. Bamboozled by his reassuring smile, dress code-approved shirt and slacks and high grade point average, the fashion police didn't know what to do with him when he arrived wearing neon orange or green socks. I had no idea where he bought neon socks; they sure weren't on the shelf where my mother shopped for school clothes.

The conservative administration, stuck in the last century, should have recognized we were over halfway through the twentieth century and let him get away with his fashion statement. They might have if he hadn't worn one of each color. The belligerent show drew a swift and certain reaction. A matador's cape to the bull, the challenge to the fashion police was obvious, and they didn't disappoint him.

Personally, I didn't appreciate his battle with authority; my proximity to his challenge put me on the administration's radar, guilt by association, my quest for invisibility annihilated. As uncomfortable as I was with a profile of any kind, I felt compelled to support my only close friend, no matter how misguided his intention.

My need for camouflage tempered support of his fashion mutiny; a pair of olive green suede Hush Puppy shoes as far out on the limb as I could go.

Alone, my shoes might have gone unnoticed, but in formation

with mismatched neon socks, the combination proved too much of an attractive nuisance.

When we walked across the outdoor spaces of the new modern campus, Eric's ankles flashed their defiant message to the staff, most of whom felt it their duty to correct the outrage. He liked nothing better than to debate the fashion guidelines with anyone foolish enough to take on his soft voice and disarming smile.

The war of wits ended before it began. He'd read the rules more carefully than the rest of us and knew there was no mention of sock color. The author of the fashion rules had also failed to antic-ipate shoes of any color other than brown or black. I checked.

An inexpensive pleasure for me, a free ride on Eric's coattails, he did all the heavy lifting in the inevitable debate, and I got to bask in the soft glow of winning.

This bit of anarchy in the face of autocratic authority was pretty tame, and the apex of trouble of which I was guilty. The admin-istrator charged with the unenviable task of enforcement of the rules was the vice principal, Mr. Neer. In two years, I experienced only one interaction with him.

In first period homeroom, general announcements were deliv-ered over the public-address system. Once in a while, some par-ticularly mischievous miscreant would receive an invitation for a visit to his office. The announcement, cousin to a public flogging, was a not-so-subtle reminder to the other inmates to avoid trou-ble. Early in the second semester of my junior year, my camouflage failed, and the ax fell on me. A cold, flat single sentence devoid of emotion delivered the invitation.

"At the end of these announcements, Mike Dennis will report to Mr. Neer's office."

Twelve hundred fellow students, less the ones who hadn't been listening, now thought I'd committed a sin worthy of his atten-tion, and I slithered out of the classroom as inconspicuously as a public calling out would allow. Audible snickering accompanied my exit.

When I arrived at his office, the ambush was already in place;

before I could announce myself, his secretary with the mirthless smile said, "He's waiting for you. You can go right in."

"Uh... thanks?"

"Close the door, take a seat." He gestured to a chair with a soft cushion that, no accident, collapsed and left me looking up at him. Nervous and confused, I fiddled with the grooves in the arms made by previous occupants and racked my mind to figure out why he'd summoned me. I didn't think I was guilty of anything he knew about.

We sat silent for what seemed an hour while his gaze shifted from me to a paper on his desk, then back. At last, he gathered his thoughts and began.

"I've been looking at your transcript. I can't figure you out. I think you're smarter than your grades. I think you're sandbagging."

He doesn't know. I'm in trouble because he thinks I'm smart?

That was really funny; I thought I was stupid. I'd never attended the same school more than two consecutive years, nine schools in twelve years, and I'd missed many of the basics necessary for understanding advanced math. Geometry made sense, but I had no idea what to do with algebra. Convinced of my ignorance and laden with guilt, I avoided math after algebra, the last required math course. I feared he'd unearthed my secret; I'd failed algebra although my transcript said I'd passed with a 'C.'

"You can go; I'll be watching you."

In the ninth grade, I crashed headlong into "New Math," a radical artifact of a failed social experiment. The Sputnik crisis of 1957 created a perceived intellectual threat from Soviet engineers who were regarded as highly skilled mathematicians. Western educators, in a panic, decided to force students to a higher standard of math and science by changing the curriculum.

They replaced algebra with a thing called Boolean Algebra.

Since no one knew how to teach it, students were supposed to learn by using a series of self-taught books.

It might have worked for someone with an adequate background in math, but for me, it was like a course in self-taught Greek. A teacher monitored the room to maintain discipline.

I failed to complete the course in the allotted time and accepted the opportunity to take the books home to finish over the summer.

Fat chance.

In the fall, the books were to be returned to the math class monitor, a teacher I liked and who shall remain nameless. Unfortunately for him I contracted a rare case of early onset dementia and for weeks, conveniently forgot to return the unfinished books in spite of his numerous reminders.

Desperate for the return of the books, the teacher said, "Look, the school says I'm responsible for those books, and they're gonna take three hundred dollars out of my next check if I don't get them back."

Too bad, Lanny.

I sympathized but had my own troubles. It may have been money out of his pocket, but I wouldn't graduate without credit for a math class I couldn't comprehend. I liked this man and wouldn't lie to him, so, with an earnest expression of incomprehension I promised once more, "I'll try to remember, sir."

His plea of financial desperation obviously hadn't produced the hoped-for result; I had the upper hand, and he knew it.

Nagging and pleading had failed, so he switched tack. Negotiation. "Okay, I get it. If you bring the books back, I'll arrange for you to get a 'C' for the class. Will that help your memory?"

Heck, yes!

Unwilling to indict myself, I nodded and muttered, "Ummmmmm."

The next day, I experienced a miraculous, spontaneous remission of dementia and cheerfully delivered the forgotten books. True to his word, he adjusted the record, and I limped through the remaining years of school, a fraud and mathematical cripple. I suffered fear and a little guilt, worried the deception would be discovered and disqualify me from graduating high school.

Graduation night, still not sure they weren't toying with me, I lined up with my classmates, crossed the stage, shook hands with the smiling principal, and accepted the silk covered binder that, when opened... was empty!

The panic was unnecessary; they were all empty. The school had avoided the awkward logistics of matching hundreds of diplomas to the correct students; the document arrived in the mail. Apparently, the school was as glad to be shed of me as I was for release from the stress of the deception.

The fallout from this educational sleight of hand hadn't been avoided, just delayed, and returned to bite years later when I purchased one of the first Computer Numerical Control milling machines sold in the Northwest.

With a contract from the state of Washington for parts I planned to make on this machine, I realized the parts were drawn in a way I couldn't use to program it.

The clever new tool had a husky monthly payment, and the contract a delivery deadline with financial penalties.

The key to deciphering the drawings was some sort of higher math and I couldn't afford to lean on the excuse, "I'm no good at math."

I went to the public library, where I knew the smart girls worked.

"Who's good at math?"

They all pointed to the same girl. I introduced myself to her, rolled out the drawings and explained my dilemma which included the truth about my qualifications, or lack thereof.

One look and she said, "You can program your machine if you can do a little trigonometry."

"Will you teach me? I'll pay."

"Sure."

Five days later, pride swallowed and digested, I had learned enough trigonometry to write the program.

Mr. Neer had been correct. I had more capability than my transcript indicated.

Startled by the increased rate our class members were passing, we decided to have a reunion every five years instead of ten. Mr. Neer was the guest of honor at the forty-five-year event.

I wanted to thank him for taking the time to challenge my lack of performance and took my place in a line of classmates, most of whom were there to express appreciation for diverting them from a life of crime. When my turn came, I shook his hand and said, "Mr. Neer, you probably don't remember me. My name is Mike Dennis. You once called me into your office, challenged me to do better, and said I was smarter than my grades suggested. You added, 'I think you're sandbagging.'

"Today, with my wife, I own a one of a kind business, hold dozens of patents, and have created more than 2,020 man-years of employment manufacturing unique products using new processes I developed from scratch.

"Seventy people currently work for us at Oregon Aero and build over seven thousand different life-saving products that are sold around the world, all because you told me you thought I wasn't stupid. Thank you!"

He stood there, still thin, ramrod straight after eighty-five years of life and hesitated a moment before responding.

Both eyebrows rose and sent ripples of wrinkles up his forehead when the enormity of his contribution to the world had sunk in.

I assumed.

You know what they say about assume.

A brief flicker of recognition and I knew he'd sorted my story from thousands of similar ones, confident he'd found my name, face, and the event in memory.

"You and that red-haired Eric kid, you two wore the goofy colored shoes and socks!"

I stood there grinning like an idiot, my balloon of self-importance burst. I was just a piece of happy flotsam in Eric's wake.

Conservative camouflage had been more effective than I realized. Mr. Neer remembered me all right, not for my untapped potential, but because I was guilty by association with my colorful friend.

Mother's Fear

Somewhere in France on a hot summer day in 1918, my grandfather and a group of American doughboys from Poulsbo, entirely confident in water, fishermen all, stripped and dived in confidently, only to discover the water was ice-cold, fast, and deep. The canal, unlike anything they'd seen at home, was steep-sided and lined with large, sharp, slippery boulders that provided little grip or purchase. They were trapped and washed along, tumbled over the rocky sides until the current, fortunately, spit them onto a low bank. Two drowned; the rest were lucky to escape with minor injuries. My mother, who never learned to swim, was traumatized by the story and never stopped talking about it. She made us promise to never swim in an irrigation ditch.

Earlier, before Eric and I discovered the dam, we had come upon friends swimming in an irrigation ditch. The water was brown, warm, and sluggish, the sides of the ditch gently sloped. "Come on in, the water's great," was an invitation I easily turned down. There's no way I was gonna have to explain to my mother how it is I drowned in an irrigation ditch.

Catcalls of "Chicken" followed us from the ditch. How could I explain my mother to them?

No irrigation ditch, a dam is entirely different and the invitation it offers is too tempting; the open spillway in the middle must be investigated.

Minutes later, chest deep in warm lake water, precariously balanced on a slimy, narrow underwater shelf, fingernails hopelessly clawed the slick, algae covered concrete. Toes, trapped in tennis shoes, curled in a reflexive but vain attempt to gain purchase when thousands of gallons of water rushed down the gaping maw of the spillway and relentlessly drew us in.

Our initial swift-paced, easy glide out to the middle of the dam was explained! This lake wasn't as still as it appeared. We'd completely missed the warning signs. The outlet was talking to us, but we couldn't hear it. Maybe we could if we'd tried but we weren't particularly interested in its message. From shore, it was only an indistinct hiss not unlike the early warning of a rattlesnake.

Two puny human bodies, overwhelmed by the mass of the moving fluid and the combined influence of buoyancy and a low coefficient of friction, obeyed the laws of physics. Our adventure was about to expand into a new, unanticipated and unknown future on the other side of the dam!

A split second before he disappeared into the outlet, Eric looked imploringly at me, and I flashed him my best "Don't worry, buddy, I'm right behind you!" look. The brave sentiment of a bug about to be sucked down a drain.

One second, I was bathed in warm, summer heat and light then, drawn by an insistent hydraulic tug, swallowed whole down the black concrete gut in one great spasm of peristalsis and swept through the absolute blackness of the dam's digestive tract where I indulged in some wishful thinking.

I wonder how long I'll be underwater? Probably not that long.

Oblivious to the obvious danger, my mind calmly awaited developments and irrationally expected a successful outcome.

Had I been wrong, we'd have just been a sad story on the front page of the Walla Walla Union-Bulletin about two really stupid kids who came to grief at the absolute apex of their combined ignorance.

If they ever found us.

We shot from the hole in wingman formation, side by side, and slid down the steep back face of the dam slippery with algae in frictionless free-fall.

22. The spillway we went through is on the right

Ahead, well, actually, down, salvation waited in the form of a large radius at the foot of the spillway that led to a long, slimy, concrete tailrace. A matched pair of fools, I could see he was thinking the same thing as me. Well, honestly, two things. First and foremost, the best news of the day, *we're not going to die!*

Secondly, *this is cool, we could do it again, on purpose, for fun!* A proof, if one is needed, of the existence of a special God who protects teenage fools. Two of his most devout parishioners practiced their catechisms in mid-flight. Even before the last act had come to its smoking conclusion, we were planning our next bit of insanity.

At the bottom, instead of a brutal, sudden stop, we smoothly swept through the radius into the tailrace where our speed failed to diminish. The water, contained in a concrete channel, maintained its velocity.

Uh, oh.

Sliding effortlessly and comfortably along the slime slick concrete, the trip through the dam's digestive tract had given us a kind of clairvoyance. We could see into our future. With this newfound prescience, a recently acquired talent for forethought (a skill that would have been useful five minutes before) we saw clearly that we definitely wouldn't be doing this again, on purpose, for fun or any other reason. Coming fast was the end of the concrete channel where the natural cobble rock riverbed began and discouraged any future plans to use the dam as a playground.

There were no fishermen standing about who might have been surprised by our sudden appearance from the face of the dam, no one to either corroborate our story or turn us in to the authorities. We were unsure whether to be disappointed by it or comforted.

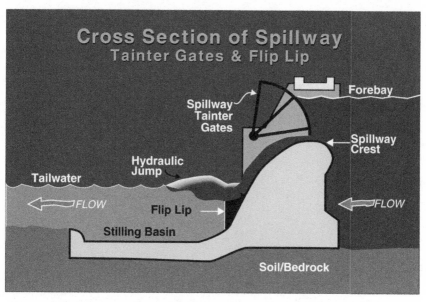

23. This is the type of spillway we went through

8.

Play Grows Up

Wa Hi, my ninth and last school before graduation, was a modern campus of handsome brick buildings connected by a spiderweb of sidewalks in an ocean of lawn bisected by Yellow Hawk Creek, and a perfect place to disappear.

Most kids had attended one of two junior high schools, so I was an outsider with no tribe, sat by myself, and listened.

"What do I need with this nonsense? I'm never gonna use the stuff they're teaching; I can't wait to get out of this hick town and move to a big city."

Wow!

I'd lived in the city they longed for and knew better. Here there was little traffic, endless opportunity to hunt, fish, hike and camp, nice people, and not enough time to do it all.

I understood their frustration with school, but rather than kick the cactus, had an idea how to change it and make it more interesting.

What this school needs is an aviation program, nothing too complicated, maybe just a private pilot ground school.

Math, physics, chemistry, geography, reading, writing, history, physical education, physiology, psychology, and socioeconomics, everything in one neat package to answer the stupid question, "How am I ever going to use this stuff in the real world?"

Honestly, I didn't care a whit for the unwashed ignorant; I wanted this for me and might be able to employ the bad attitude as an ally.

The world was an angry place in 1967. Anti-war sentiment fractured the country, the 'generation gap' grew wider; students were 'us' and school boards, part of the hated establishment, 'them.'

No one likes to be hated. Maybe I can manipulate their desire to be liked.

I'd done my homework, knew the financial condition of the school district, found a qualified teacher with time in his schedule interested in a ground school, and talked to the head of building services who showed me an empty room in the science building.

Armed with answers to all the objections I could anticipate, I presented myself and my idea at the next school board meeting. My pitch for a ground school was received with the usual enthusiasm for a new idea.

"NO!"

Innocently, I asked, "Why?"

"No money," said the richest school district in the state, one with a surplus.

Check!

"What would you need money for?"

"Well, son, you don't understand. A new class like this is just too expensive. We'd need to pay a teacher, fund a classroom, and purchase the books, supplies, and training aids."

"You need a teacher, a classroom, the books, and stuff? That's it? That's everything?"

"Yes, that's about it."

Checkmate.

"Okay. Thanks for considering my proposal. See you next month."

I turned to leave and heard over my shoulder, "What's he talking about, see you next month?"

I didn't figure NO meant no since they qualified it with an explanation, and I assumed it was a positive response if I could figure out how to acquire the books and supplies. I already had everything else.

In the sixth grade, I'd learned the power of the "Ask" when we wrote a letter to the Bic Pen Company and asked for some of their new, novel, colored ballpoint pens for an art project. A tiny school in the desert, twelve kids in the sixth grade, we had lots of creativity, but no money. Two weeks later three hundred colored pens were delivered to the school.

That's it? Just ask? Cool!

A masterpiece of creative writing, I crafted a letter to the Sanderson Company, the leader in pilot training courses, and asked for their help. I might have made it sound like there was more enthusiasm for the idea than existed in reality, but without the books, there was no chance.

Three weeks later a truck arrived at our house with thirty cases of everything a student needed for a ground school accompanied by a very nice letter of encouragement for the 'program.'

The Sting

"What have you got there?" asked Dad as he got out of his car behind me. He knew nothing of my plan.

"Ah, yeah, I sorta went to the last school board meeting and asked them to think about offering a ground school course in the high school."

"What'd they say?"

"They said they didn't have the money."

"Yeah, they would, did they say what they'd need it for?"

"Well, you know, a teacher, classroom, books, and training aids."

"I see you've got the books. Do you have the teacher and classroom?"

"Yup."

"I assume you intend to go to the next board meeting."

"Yup."

"You do know, don't you, they aren't gonna be happy being ambushed. I think you need some help; I'll come too, but don't introduce me. I'll arrive late and sit in the back of the room. Ignore me."

"Why?"

"Just do it."

"Okay."

I'm no fool.

At the next school board meeting, I introduced Mr. Bowman, the shop teacher who'd agreed to teach the class and Mr. Smith, the building services manager, who offered, "We have an empty classroom in the science building, and I can't tell you what a great idea this is of yours. My kid is ready to sign up as soon as the course is available."

I might have given him the impression I was just the gopher, doing their bidding.

Then, clatter, bang, thump, Dad came through the door at the back of the room like clumsy Columbo. Dressed in his Sunday best, he sat at a desk, opened his briefcase, snap, snap, then ceremoniously removed a notebook and pen, obviously ready to record every word of the meeting. He looked up, smiled at the board, and clicked the pen several times for effect.

The board hemmed and hawed while Dad wrote furiously in his notebook every time someone spoke, but the war was over without a shot. There would be an aeronautics course offered in the fall.

I took the course the next semester; the final exam was a trip to the local FAA flight service station to sit for the private pilot written test. Eighty-seven percent of the class passed.

No one would describe me as 'a good student.' Proud of my perfect record (in four years of high school, I'd never taken a book home) I shocked everyone with a ninety-six. I went on and talked myself into the assistant instructor job where I built training aids and demonstration models the second semester. It was the best year of my high school experience.

One year later, I earned my pilot's license.

Five decades after my check-ride, I've logged eight thousand hours as a pilot, and in collaboration with a local university, the high school offers flight training and courses in aviation management with college credit, as well as the ground school.

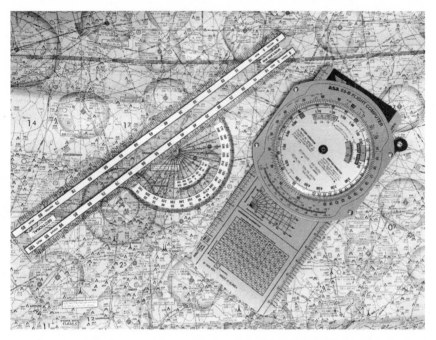

24. *Chart, plotter, and E6B, an example of some of the aviation ground school supplies needed for our class.*

9.

Counsel of Last Resort

"I hope you know how wonderful your parents are," was a line I got once in a while spoken in hushed and reverential tones from a schoolmate, usually a girl I knew, but not well. Not a question, and not actually concerned that I didn't appreciate my parents, what she really meant was, "Your father is wonderful."

Oh, I'm so sorry. You have my condolences.

She didn't know it, but I'd broken the code. If my father was in her life as closely as her admonition implied, there must be real trouble in the house.

At first flattered, I thought it was a come-on, but couldn't figure out why. I was new to the school, cute enough, (handsome would be overstating it) but not a part of the connected social fabric of a city with a decidedly polarized financial magnetic field.

One pole, old money, wheat-farm wealthy, (a ten-thousand-acre farm was only interesting); the other, people who owned the businesses. Everyone else, the field that connected the poles. I hovered someplace on a lower rung of the last category, knew it, and didn't care. I liked the life I'd built for myself and looked forward to more of the same in the future.

So why the message?

Because sometimes, even the pillars of a community need someone to talk to. My dad, with his innate ability to connect with everyone except the people who lived under his roof, was the court-appointed someone.

If the upper crust, and I call them that with respect, had personal issues bigger than they could handle by themselves, and who doesn't from time to time, he was who they turned to, or were sent to because of his absolute discretion. A secret shared with him was as safe as cash in a bank vault. If there were a leak, it came from fissures in the family of interest like my school friends, not him.

The small garage off the alley behind the house, out of view of the neighbors, doubled as a workshop where I maintained my rolling fleet. Expensive cars, out of place in the neighborhood, often occupied the driveway while their owners, my concerned classmates' parents, traversed the outside stairway to Dad's upstairs office. Through a window in the garage, I had a front-row seat to the show.

Although the exact nature of his interactions with the clientele was none of my business and I didn't care to pry, his hidden influence on the magnetic field would ripple into the future and have a profound, direct, and positive effect on me.

Just One of His Germans

Meanwhile, back at the German bakery...

"You kids go outside and wait on the curb. I'll just be a few minutes," he commanded.

Minutes turned into hours whiled away on the sidewalk. When he finally emerged, I'd ask, "Wha'd you guys talk about?"

His answer, an obvious lie, "Oh, they're just lonesome for Germany and want to speak German to someone," shed no light.

Sure they do.

No matter how curious the anarchist in my head, I knew not to push.

These chance encounters happened so often we considered them "normal." The evening of my high school commencement, our family went to dinner at a local steakhouse to celebrate. The waitress came to the table, looked at Dad, let out a scream, dropped her pencil and pad, and fled. Everyone in the place turned to watch when he tipped over his chair to run after her.

We let the communal curiosity cool, then I told Mother, "I'll go see what's up." I found them in the kitchen sitting on a pair of milk crates, embroiled in an emotional conversation in German.

"It's just one of his Germans," I told the family when I returned. They nodded, and another waiter took our order. We had finished dinner before Dad came back, ordered, ate in silence, and looked through the table with his post-encounter, thousand-yard stare.

Emboldened by my recent escape from adolescence, I pushed.

"I'm not ten years old anymore; what was that really about?"

I think he'd forgotten we were there, or maybe it just didn't matter, but the question broke his reverie and, startled, he answered, "Oh, a long time ago, I arrested her brother, and she thinks I'm here to arrest her."

"What did you tell her?"

"I said, it was another time, and she had nothing to fear from me."

It sounds like an answer.

Two Plus Two Equals...?

This game of cat and mouse had been going on for a long time. Adults underestimate the computing power of a kid who is little more than an information sponge with a vast amount of time to process what he sees and hears. I'd always been hugely curious about the things and people who came before me and would formulate questions designed to expand small bits of data such as, "What do you mean you worked on a ship, what kind?"

"A cable laying ship, Mikie."

"What's that?"

Sigh. "It's a ship that lays long-distance phone cable on the bottom of the sea so we can talk to people far away."

I know that.

I'd seen a TV program about the ships that laid transatlantic cables while they plowed through scary-looking seas, but I had him talking and wanted to keep him going, so I asked more questions for which I knew the answer.

"Was the weather bad, was it cold, were the waves big, was it scary?"

"Yes, the weather was bad, and yes it was freezing. We used sledgehammers to chip ice from the ship; too much weight on top and she could roll over."

He glanced up to the left to retrieve a little more information. "Yes, the waves were huge, sometimes they washed clear over the ship, and yes I was scared. I was just the cabin boy."

"But, but, you're old, how could you be a cabin boy?" I stammered. It was too late; there'd be no more answers, he'd turned and walked away.

Age perspective is an acquired skill.

In 1957, while sitting around the metaphorical campfire, my friends, hungry to associate themselves with derring-do would ask, "Wha'd your dad do in the war?" One might say, "My dad was a ball turret gunner in a bomber," and another, "Mine landed on Omaha Beach." I longed to have a story to tell and improvised, emphasizing the danger of an ice-sheathed ship and the balance required to carry a tray of coffee mugs across a slippery, heaving deck.

Later, with a more sophisticated picture of history, I asked him, "Where were you on December 7, 1941, when the Japanese bombed Pearl Harbor?"

Proud that I'd figured out he might have been in harm's way, (I mean, where'd his German language skill come from?) I expected a harrowing tale of battle.

Maybe he fought off hordes of Zeros with an anti-aircraft gun, or cleverly ensnared an enemy submarine in the underwater cable. Maybe, he was a spy.

"Setting pins in a bowling alley."

Whaaaat the heck? Working in a bowling alley? What about the cable ship, the guns, the Zeros, and the Germans?

The bowling alley answer, wildly inconsistent with my expectation, was so unacceptable I pushed it into the back of my mind and conveniently forgot it.

Meanwhile, otherworldly encounters with shocked Germans piled up and my curiosity increased. I peppered him with questions until he explained away his knowledge of German and the strangers who recognized him on sight with a story that was, like the best lies, short, and mostly true.

"During World War Two, along with others, I volunteered for a special mission. We were taught German and trained in unarmed hand-to-hand combat. The plan was to parachute behind German lines before D-Day and cause as much mayhem and disruption as possible by attacking their command structure's communications and personnel. I arrived in England too late for the drop, so they sent me to France to work with Army Intelligence to search out and arrest German war criminals."

I tried to digest this information, place it in the context of derring-do and combat but had trouble doing so.

"Okay, so no fighting, no gunfire. You fought the war with a clipboard and what, a badge that said, Special Bad Guy Cop?"

"Yeah, that's about it, all right."

In time, I found his story contained a patina of truth. The program, "Operation Jedburgh," was so secret it remained in the shadows of history for decades. The men were taught to use improvised weapons in close-quarter combat but, unlike my father, they did not learn German; they spoke it already.

June 6, 1944, D-Day, he was only seventeen and a half.

10.

Higher Education

Eighteen the summer of '68, I'd graduated high school, had a handful of hours in my precious flight log, but many more spent in the cracked leather seat of an engineless Piper Cub I'd found abandoned behind a hangar. Faded yellow, rotten fabric hung from it in tatters.

Warm sunlight filtered through the cataract of its crazed plastic windshield, a gentle breeze rocked the wings, and my imagination provided the view.

Like an addict, I inhaled the sweet perfume of brake fluid, engine oil, avgas, dope, and the musty odor of sweat from a thousand frightened students; a narcotic that could induce a nap with the quality of a coma. I dreamed of a life to come.

All I need now is to complete my flying lessons as soon as possible.

As a benefit of the aviation ground school class, I'd passed the private pilot written exam with a score of ninety-six. With no experience, I'd missed the two confusing-as-a-foreign-language questions about radio phraseology. In light of my academic performance to date, my parents were hard pressed to comprehend the achievement.

Even though I'd created the class and attended as a student, then the teacher's assistant, I had no idea how to begin a career in aviation. My successful written exam would be good for two years. I needed forty hours or more of expensive flight training, or I'd have to retake the written. With my perishable academic skill, I was motivated to get the job done.

When I tried to talk with Mother about my aviation aspirations, she claimed to be terrified of the idea and refused to talk about it.

I pushed her. "What do you think?"

Certain her logic to be unassailable, she blurted, "Forget it! You've got champagne taste on a beer budget!"

Blinded by my aviation addiction, oddly, I received her sentiment as a compliment.

Nice! Mother thinks I have good taste and the sense to have a budget.

Dad, sympathetic but practical, kept his opinion to himself. I believe he was afraid of the expense and, possibly, Mother, and was in no position to render cash or consolation, so he offered neither.

The heading of my life had been set when I'd received a 'Divine Message'; however, the force of life's circumstances had conspired to make the course difficult. Dad's chosen career path as a country preacher made his financial participation impossible so, as a matter of practical expediency, when I was eight I joined the ranks of the self-employed and began mowing lawns to earn my own money.

We never confronted the issue head-on, but ten years later I understood, at summer's end, my parents expected me to leave home and make my own way, college their preferred path, but I wasn't so sure.

I'd traded many weeks of farm work at minimum wage, a dollar sixty-five an hour, less taxes and social security, for half a dozen flying lessons that vacuumed up cash at the breathtaking rate of eighteen dollars an hour.

Money for flight instruction flowed like water going downhill. Aviation, shockingly expensive, was worth every penny.

My underwhelming bank account was also the casualty of an inclination to buy, build, and fuel a fleet of vehicles. For economical local transportation, I'd built an expensive fifteen-speed bicycle, had acquired an old black and white Honda 250 motorcycle to get to the farm, and inherited a fuel-thirsty, blue and white 1955 Chevy Wagon from Dad, who'd bought it new. For long-distance economy travel, I overhauled and re-upholstered a red 1964 Volkswagen Beetle.

Each machine had been progressively more expensive to buy, rebuild and operate, and now I intended to dive headlong into aviation, the most expensive motor pool of all. In retrospect, my mother's observation of "Champagne taste on a beer budget," was spot-on.

25. Dad and me

26. Me, mom, and Dad's dog Tuffy on my high school graduation day

What savings I had were set aside to pay the modest bill at a small liberal arts college, a school almost foolish enough to accept me and my questionable academic record.

I had no business attending a liberal arts school, a course of study I didn't like, that didn't suit me. It wasn't much of a plan. I was just following a crowd of friends, and the college hadn't actually accepted me yet.

They were still thinking it over.

For four years, I'd lived and worked on the small farm thirty miles from home; full time in the summer, and as much time as possible in the winter. Now I was on the way to meet my family on the Oregon Coast for one last vacation before leaving home for good.

I stopped by our empty house in Walla Walla to pack a bag, found a letter from the college on the kitchen table, opened it and discovered they'd finally come to their senses.

Dear Mr. Dennis,

Thank you again for your interest in continuing your education with us here at 'Podunk University'. We have received your application, academic record, and letter of recommendation from your aviation sciences instructor, but our admissions board has determined we will also require a letter from one of your liberal arts instructors.

There it was, the jig was up, someone smelled an academic rat and wanted an appropriate teacher to perjure himself to get me into their college.

I stood in my mother's familiar kitchen and a flame of self-sufficient indignation spontaneously ignited in my brain.

Enough of this farce!

With malice aforethought, first-degree murder of my academic future, I opened the cupboard under the sink, dropped the letter into the trash, walked out the front door and began the six-hour drive to the beach.

The college would never miss me.

On the drive, a single thought loomed large; the instant I'd trashed my ill-conceived educational scheme, I'd also abandoned my college deferment and left myself vulnerable to the military draft.

'The Draft,' a familiar but vague reality before, suddenly had become a fact of life and I was now eligible. Six hours of driving, enough time to consider what that might mean for my immediate future clarified my thoughts and, by the time I got to the beach, I had a new plan.

I'm gonna get my life back on track, and to avoid the unpleasant possibility of being drafted into the foot soldier army, I'll go see that Army recruiter.

"Son, you never mind those stuck-ups at the Air Force who won't let you fly without a college degree. The U.S. Army would be delighted to teach you to fly helicopters, a valuable skill you can use later... if you survive."

I missed his not-so-subtle message about the possible undesirable consequences; "Free Flight Training," the only thing I heard. The Army's generous offer had a catch. In appreciation of the opportunity, they required a four-year hitch and a tour or two in exotic places like Vietnam where one in three helicopter pilots didn't survive.

In light of my recent scholastic change of plan, I wasn't all that anxious to reunite with the family and have to answer their inevitable question.

"So, now that you've graduated high school, what are your plans?"

Mother already thought I was out of my mind to want to do something as "dangerous" as fly airplanes. She was gonna really love my new idea.

To delay the inevitable, I retreated to the Conference Center kitchen where my friend, Mrs. Rice, the head cook, was pleased to see me. We got along well because when I'd worked for her, I demonstrated respect for adults, enjoyed work, used scalding hot water to wash the pots and pans, and would get up at three in the morning to bake the bread, muffins, and sweet rolls. She also appreciated my expertise with a steel to put a razor-sharp edge on her kitchen knives.

After a short visit, Mrs. Rice returned to her dinner preparation, and I continued to restore an edge to her knives. Much practice allowed me the luxury of operating on autopilot as the knife flashed back and forth over the steel, "zick, zick, zick."

I noticed a small white book at the bottom of a nearby trash can. Curious, I put the knife and steel down, leaned over, and fished out a book the size of a Reader's Digest. Obviously a low-budget effort, it had no pictures, just simple black text on a white cover: LeTourneau College.

Whatever that is.

In 1946, Mr. R.G. LeTourneau, inventor of the world's largest earthmoving equipment, purchased Harmon General Hospital, a former military facility, two-hundred buildings on fifty-six acres in Longview, Texas.

A man with a broad vision, Mr. R.G. intended to build an engineering and technical school where he would educate GIs who had begun to return from duty in World War II.

Ho hum, so far so good.

Twenty-two years later, the school offered four-year degrees in engineering and two-year associate degrees in various fields of technology like Machine Tool, Welding, Automotive, Electrical, Electronics, something called Computer Science, and Aviation Maintenance.

Holy cow! An aviation school! Who knew?

After two years in the aviation program, a graduate will have an Airframe and Power Plant Mechanic license and, if he wants, can continue for another two years and receive a degree in Aeronautical Engineering.

Dang! Two birds with one rock. The engineering degree would be a long shot with my shaky math skills but, who knows, anything is possible.

The school had been custom designed for someone like me.

Why had no one told me a school like this existed? For a moment, I reconsidered my college aspirations until I turned the page and the world of aviation the book promised vanished like a mirage, and Mother's words came back to haunt me.

Aviation is expensive! The tuition for the aircraft maintenance program, five thousand a semester, is more money than Dad makes in a year.

For perspective, gasoline had just shot up to the ridiculous price of thirty-four cents a gallon.

Stunned by the tuition, I turned the page and had salt rubbed into the financial wound by a breathtaking list of expensive and required tools.

The more I read, the worse things got; classes began in two weeks, and freshmen weren't allowed to work or bring a car. If by some miracle the obstacles could be overcome, the no-car rule swept up the only affordable way I could get myself to a school half a continent away.

The impossible requirements accumulated, compounded, and extinguished the small flame that had begun to burn in my mind. Preoccupied with the book, I didn't notice someone walk up and quietly stand behind me.

"Watcha looking at, Mike?"

I recovered from the surprise and recognized Donna P., the director of the girls who worked on the dining room staff.

"A book," I stammered, unable to tear myself away long enough to look at her.

"A book about what?"

"Ah... well, I'm not sure, I think it's a college catalog, but I've never seen one like it."

"Do you see a course in it that interests you?"

"Yes, yes, I sure do," I responded enthusiastically then, armed with minutes-old expertise in the education offered by the school, babbled on about the aviation program and how it fit my lifelong addiction to aviation.

"Well then, that's where you should go."

Right! Stupid woman, you don't have a clue. It's not as simple as deciding to go.

I knew better than to let a thought like that loose. Instead, in a tone one might reserve for a particularly dull child, I answered, "No, I don't think so. It's too expensive, requires a long list of tools I can't afford, begins in two weeks, is halfway across the country, and won't allow freshmen to work or have a car, so I couldn't get there in time, anyway."

She repositioned herself, stood in front of me where she could see my face and, unmoved by my explanation of a dream that had drifted out of reach, persisted.

In her own 'how stupid can you be?' tone, she enunciated one word at a time. "Yes, I understand all of that. Listen carefully to the question. Do. You. Want. To. Go. There?"

Man! Either you don't get it, or you're some sort of sadist. I'm an optimist, but can't you see? The shimmering future is a bus that already slid into the ditch.

Determined to end the agony and terminate the insane conversation, I looked her in the eye and called her cruel bluff.

"Okay, yes! Sure, I want to attend the school!"

There, evil person, deal with that!

Unperturbed, she smiled and countered, "Then come with me."

She turned, walked out the door and, in her wake, the sharp slam of the screen door echoed through the kitchen. Surprised, but trained to respect my elders, I slid off the stool and followed.

In a weak attempt to regain the upper hand in a conversation that had cascaded out of control, I called, "Where we go'n?" Several paces ahead of me, she didn't so much as turn her head to answer.

"Bruce's."

The bizarre response floated back to where I struggled to maintain my teenage cool.

"Bruce's? The... candy... store?"

"Yes."

Decades before cell phones, one of two payphones in Cannon Beach hung in a glass and aluminum phone booth on the south end of Bruce's Candy Kitchen. Beside the booth, Donna said, "You wait here," then stepped inside and closed the door. She used a calling card to pay for a call.

Cool. I've heard of those but never seen one. I wonder what she's up to?

While she talked, I watched the taffy machine in the window of Bruce's go around and soaked in the rare warmth of a sunny day on the chronically cloudy coast.

The jury in my mind that adjudicated such things decided Donna's "you stay here" instruction allowed me the latitude to pace in circles and kick up clouds of dust with my toe while I waited.

For what, I had no idea but sensed something important was happening. Broken by the wicked scrape of the phone booth door, the spell ended abruptly.

27. The phone booth outside Bruce's Candy Kitchen

"There, you're all signed up. We'd better go talk to your folks."

She turned on one heel and began a quick march back to the Conference Center.

What the hell!

Caught off guard, I stood there slack-jawed, surrounded by the shards of my shattered composure, and watched her walk away.

"What? Wait a minute! Signed up for what?"

"Your first semester at LeTourneau," she said over her shoulder.

"My what?"

What's wrong with you? I already explained, I can't afford the school.

Befuddled, I asked the only question I could think of.

"How do I pay for it?"

Her answer did little to unbefuddle me.

"You don't; it's all paid for."

Paid for? What the hell is she talking about?

"Who are you, really?"

"You mean when I'm not the director of the wait staff here in the summer?"

"Yes."

"I'm the Women's residence hall supervisor at LeTourneau."

You're kidding!

As if it made any difference, I asked, "Where does the money come from?"

"The College has a grant fund for missionary and preacher's kids. We know you get a mixed bag of education while your family moves around, so we admit you no questions asked and pay for your first semester.

"After that, it's up to you. Maintain your grades, and you can qualify for additional grants. There's plenty of money if you work hard. Let's go talk to your folks; you have a lot to do and not much time to get it done."

I'd been making all my own decisions since I was fourteen. Fate, or something else, and this woman had mauled my eighteen-year-old ego, played a trump card, and swept my decision control from the table.

She'd presented me with an unearned, unimaginable opportunity that had nothing to do with my sterling character, only a result of my father's random choice of a career.

Get over it, Ace, you're going to airplane school!

Nonplussed, Dad listened to my story, how I tossed the school's letter in the trash, my decision to fly helicopters for the Army, the catalog, and now, Donna's new plan. Mother, unsure whether my story was good news or bad, asked, "What does he mean, fly for the Army?"

I glanced at Dad, and his eyes said, *don't talk.*

"It's good news, dear," he said and didn't bother to explain the military consequences of scrapping my previous college plan. He understood as well as I did how the draft worked and knew it wasn't necessary to burden her with the details of my latest idea for coping with Selective Service.

He read a couple of pages in the little white book, looked up and said, "Get your stuff together. We need to drive home and see Hubert."

Three-hundred-fifty miles later, he and I went to the hardware store Hubert operated with his son Neil. Hubert, a deacon in Dad's current church, had been in the hardware business for fifty years. Dad handed him the list of tools and gave the book to Neil.

"Hubert, Mike's going to airplane school. We need this stuff."

A man of few words, Hubert looked at the list and grunted once.

"Come with me."

The events of the last two days had improved my attitude; I followed Hubert while Neil skimmed the book, excused himself, and disappeared out the front door. In the back room of his old store, under a work bench, Hubert opened big wooden drawers and began filling a new toolbox with tools.

"These aren't just new tools. These are some of the best tools ever made. See, they're old, new tools, salesman's samples I collected over the last half-century. Ya can't buy better ones."

"I can't afford them, Hubert."

"Are ya stupid or what? I didn't pay nothin' for 'um, and you won't, either."

He was right, and half a century later, I still own them all. We found every tool on the list except one with a funny name, a tool unique to aviation. Cleco pliers are used to install and remove a temporary sheet metal fastener called, appropriately enough, a cleco.

When I got to school, I found them for sale in the bookstore for $3.50. They knew no one would find a pair in a hardware store.

After the tools were boxed up, the bell on the front door tinkled brightly. Neil walked in, smiled, and handed me an envelope.

"I read where they won't let you drive a car to school. You don't have much time to get there, so you'll need this."

Another miracle conjured from thin air, but thick with generosity, the envelope contained a one-way airline ticket from Pendleton, Oregon, to Longview, Texas.

It had been less than forty-eight hours since Donna said, "Come with me."

I would arrive in Longview a week early with three hundred pounds of new tools, a fresh military deferment, and a paid-for first semester.

The unexpected alteration in my life's course vaporized my Army helicopter pilot future faster than I'd dreamed it up.

Probably for the best.

Three days later, I waited for my first airline flight, and a four-engine United Airlines DC-6 waited for me on the ramp, gleaming silver in the sun.

My family stood quietly in the terminal while Dad delivered a short sermon, an admonition for me to do well, then fell into stoic Scandinavian silence. Still as a statue on the outside, a frantic mess on the inside, I prepared to leave home for the last time.

We don't do tears.

Pre-TSA, we walked outside to the ramp where the gate agent took my ticket and, no fanfare, I climbed the boarding stairway and took my seat. Alone, my stern Norse heritage abandoned me, and I pressed my face to the little window and waved at their backs as my family walked away.

One down, four to go, I guess.

The stewardess stood and closed the passenger door on the outside world and, metaphorically, on my childhood.

28. I took this picture from the DC-6 leaving Pendleton

Broken clouds obscured much of the view.
We must be about over Haines.

When we were kids, no cell phones, video games, television or radio to occupy us, my brother Jim and I would lie in our yard and wait for the Salt Lake City-bound United flight to pass over.

Unlike a jet, the DC-6 crawled slowly across the dome of sky and flew low enough for us to see the polished aluminum glitter in the sun. Mesmerized by the delicious baritone drone of its piston engines, we imagined where the lucky passengers were going.

There!

Through a hole in the clouds, I could see one of the valley's distinctive mushroom-shaped haystacks. Loose hay had been forked inside a circular fence until the pile overflowed.

We're close.

No sooner than I thought it, Haines appeared in the window at the base of the Elkhorn Mountains.

There's the house, the church, and Daryl's house with the dark green circle of grass we planted in the pasture for a flying field.

I discovered another miracle of flight as we flew over the place my airplane passion had bloomed into full flower.

Jules Verne was right; time machines are real.

The view of a familiar place from altitude is recognizable but fuzzy; memory fills in the detail.

Cool! From here, I can see into my childhood, and if I look close enough, I'm sure I can see two boys lying in the grass.

Without warning, tears, happy tears, brimmed and spilled down my face.

I'm on my way to airplane school, flying in my first airliner over the very place aviation came alive for me.

As overwhelming as it was, it was about to get even more interesting.

Embarrassed by my emotional reaction, I kept my face turned to the window so the stewardess wouldn't see. I needn't have worried.

She had issues of her own and the sound of sniffling made me aware that someone occupied the previously empty seat beside me. My melancholy evaporated when I turned to find her, crying.

Yipes! I have no idea what to do with this.

Raised to behave like a gentleman, I did the best I could.

"Hello. Are you all right?"

"I'll be okay." She sniffled and blew her nose. "This is an emotional flight for the crew."

"Why?"

"This is the last piston-powered flight of a scheduled United Airlines airplane. When we land in Salt Lake, this plane will go to the wreckers, and we'll be an 'All Jet Fleet'."

With a wistful glance, she took in the familiar cabin then said, "And you're the last passenger."

I followed her lead and, for the first time, looked around the aircraft.

By golly, she's right; the last, because I'm the only one.

Dale Crane

Someone had tacked the 'Intake Interview' list on the bulletin board outside the cafeteria; mine was at 1:30 with Dale Crane in his office in the aviation building.

Good timing. I have just enough time to stop by the bookstore and pick up my textbooks.

I set the stack of heavy books on a chair outside his office, then knocked on the door.

"Come in, please. Take a chair. Make yourself comfortable."

"Thank you, Sir."

He's a lot older than I expected.

"You can drop the sir, just call me Mr. Crane."

"Okay, Sir... ah, Mr. Crane."

Dale Crane was the Director of Aviation at LeTourneau College and I could tell where his questions were headed. He wanted to understand my motivation for attending. Did I think aviation sounded like something cool, or was I serious?

You have no idea, Sir. I'm serious as a heart attack.

Behind him was a bookcase. On top was the fuselage of an old, large model airplane with the wings removed. I'd built a number of planes like that. To transport the model, the wings were held on with stout rubber bands and easy to remove.

After twenty minutes of conversation, Dale looked me in the eye and pointed up.

"What's that?"

Without breaking eye contact, I answered.

"A Rearwin Speedster tandem two seat with inline Menasco C-4 engine, not a Sportster, also a tandem two seat but powered most often with an 85-90 hp LeBlond radial, and definitely not a Cloudster, a two-place side by side powered by a selection of fully cowled, Ken-Royce radials. Rae Rearwin and his two sons, Ken and Royce, founded the company."

He looked at me evenly for a moment, then nodded.

"You'll do."

Nice! The best compliment I ever got.

I built the models from plastic kits at a workbench in the back of Dad's office. The history came from books at the library.

I'd read them all. Twice.

After the interview, I hoisted the load of books (that I later learned were common to every aviation school in the country) from the chair and one slid off the stack. I picked it up and noticed the author's name on the spine. Crane.

Yup, that one.

Rules are to be Broken

Employed continuously since I was eight, school life without a job quickly became impossible. Most everyone I knew had parents who sent them regular support checks.

That isn't gonna happen for me.

Someone told me the head of the Aviation Power Plant Lab needed an assistant, so I made a beeline for his office where I found his name on the little sign on the door, Roger Carr. I knocked.

"Come in."

"Hello, Mr. Carr, my name is Mike. I understand you need an

assistant. I'd like to apply for the job. Hire me; you'll never regret it."

"What do you know how to do, Mike?"

"What do you need, Sir?"

"Really, you can do anything I need?"

29. My first solo, Longview, Texas, April 19, 1969

"No, Sir, I know how to do a lot of things, but if I don't, I know how to find someone who does, and if I can't, I'll figure it out."

"Where'd you come from?"

"The farm, Sir. I ran a small one by myself. If I didn't get something done, it didn't get done. Everything got done, Sir."

"You're a freshman. Freshmen aren't supposed to have a job."

"I've thought about that, Sir, I believe the rule was put in place because jobs are in town. It takes a lot of time to get back and forth and is impossible without a car. The Lab is right here, Sir. I can be here in two minutes, work, then be back in the dorm as quickly. I'd be working instead of watching television like so many others. Who else has asked for the job?"

114

I've got you there.

"What do you need the money for?"

"I need to finish my flight training. Working part-time for you, I'd earn nineteen dollars and fifty cents a week; lessons cost eighteen dollars an hour. The extra dollar and a half, I'd use to buy dinner on Sundays when the cafeteria is closed."

"What are you doing for dinner now?"

"I don't eat on Sunday night, Sir."

He gave me the job.

30. R.G. LeTourneau and me checking out one of his earth movers

I cashed the check, hitchhiked to the Greg County Airport, and gave the FBO eighteen dollars. Carlos Diaz, my first flight instructor, gave me an hour of instruction, after which I hitchhiked to the Burger King, bought dinner, and walked back to school. Every week.

It was heaven, and Roger was my angel.

Money

"It's easier for a camel to go through the eye of a needle than for a rich man to enter Heaven" is an oft-quoted biblical admonition.

Flying is expensive; I'm gonna need a lot of the stuff.

On a rare Sunday when I paid attention to his sermon, Dad neutralized the moral dilemma with a history lesson.

"The quote is an aberration of the writer's words; the impossibility of a camel passing through the eye of a needle is obvious.

"People have distorted the passage to disparage the appreciation of money, but the author had no such intention, rather the opposite. In the context of the time, the rich man in the audience would understand his message; entrance into Heaven, for any man, requires humility.

"The city of the time, surrounded by a wall for reasons of security, couldn't afford to open and close the main gate for every peddler. To allow commerce, the wall had several small, low gates that required the merchant to bow low, his camel to kneel and walk through on its knees. Inside the gate stood a pair of guards with large swords ready to separate an enemy from his head if he tried to enter the city.

"The gate had a name. The 'Needle's Eye.'"

The Pilot

"His name is Irv; he's a pilot!"

Instantly, Dad had my undivided, ten-year-old attention.

"Who's a pilot?"

"Irv. I met him at Camp Silver Creek. He has a Stinson, he and his wife are going to the Philippines, he's a missionary pilot, and he took me up in his airplane."

That explains where he's been. Dad has a new friend with a plane, and they went flying without me. Grrrrr.

Two years later, I forgave both of them when Irv came to our church to raise the money for work in the Philippines. It would take the combined efforts of a lot of churches to get it done.

"Crime in Baguio is a problem. Everyone over there says we need a guard dog."

I can do that.

"Mr. Irv, Sir, I think the kids here can raise the money for a dog."

Maybe they can, maybe not, but I just volunteered them. For a collection bank, I built a model of his Stinson 108, cut a slot in the top, shook down everyone who would listen and asked each for a quarter until we had enough to buy a German Shepard puppy.

Irv had watched us fly model planes in the backyard... and understood. One day while visiting my friend Steve at his home in Portland, Irv, who lived in the area, called.

"You boys want to go fly? I'll come get you and we'll drive to Beaverton then fly to Hillsboro to pick up some parts."

He put me in the left seat for the round trip, fifteen minutes in each direction. Age twelve, my first lesson, and already an enthusiast, I shamelessly became a lifelong airplane addict.

He didn't need to fly; it would have taken him an hour to drive to Hillsboro and back, less time than it took to drive into Portland and pick us up.

My Dad's friend Irv arranged my first job at an airport, taught me to fly ("It's easy, keep the dirty side down, the clean side up, and the pointy end forward") at no cost, changed my life forever, and became a lifelong friend. We flew together for the next fifty years until, age eighty-four, he flew West, and I give rides to anyone interested.

31. Irv and me with my Navion Rangemaster

11.

The Champ

The popular belief that western Oregon is beset with a year-round temperate rain that falls from a perpetual overcast is inaccurate. Western Oregon has four seasons. During the seven-month "Rainy Season," the large black arrow on the "FIRE DANGER" sign outside the U.S. Forest Service office gathers moss and robs the sign's dramatic intent with its simple message, "None."

In December and January, the "Flood Season," your morning commute might require a boat. Dense grass and shrubs that proliferate in the damp seasons become the fuel for August and September, the "Fire Season."

That leaves July. The short but dependable "Summer Season" was putting on a show. A warm west breeze rolled vaporous tumbleweeds of fair weather cumulus across a blue sky.

An airplane mechanic for an upstart little aviation company, new to the job in the summer of 1972 and victim of workplace politics, all outdoor maintenance was mine. The senior mechanic, who'd been there three months longer than me, accomplished out-of-the-weather work under an open garage door inside an unheated shack. We were both cold in the Rainy Season, but I was often wet, too. So happy to be working at an airport again, I forgot the miserable chill and damp with the first full day of sunshine.

On my back in the gravel, inspecting a nose wheel assembly for a crack, came a far-away hum of a horde of insects. The buzz grew into the unmistakable roar of a World War II, four-engine B-17 bomber. As curious as the rest, I crawled from under the plane to join a crowd of hangar rats who searched the eastern sky certain a rare treat approached, a Flying Fortress.

Patiently we waited and waited... then waited some more. Although the drone continued, it didn't seem to get any closer until the machine responsible for the fearsome noise appeared over the tree line, and the crowd groaned. Not a B-17, but a brand-spanking-new Bellanca Champ. Underpowered by a worthless, unbelievably noisy two-cylinder Franklin engine, it made little headway into the breeze.

Aeronca, long since departed from the small aircraft scene, designed the Model 7 Champion, 'Champ'. Bellanca Aircraft bought the type certificate, installed the low-cost engine and began to manufacture the tailwheel two-seat trainer from a bygone era.

Our employer had told us the Champ was on the way. They planned to use this new machine to do the impossible, go back in time; fly, literally, in the face of the insurance company and offer tailwheel instruction to pilots who had never flown an airplane without a nose wheel.

I planned to be first.

One hundred hours in my log book, half the flights were less than three-tenths of an hour; short hops around the pattern to warm the oil before maintenance. I'd flown fourteen different aircraft types and intended to make this number fifteen.

I'd fly anything and hadn't learned that some airplanes are better left un-flown.

Before the machine made its way downwind to land, I ran into the office and signed up for an hour of dual with our tailwheel instructor, Ace. The day we met he smiled, extended a hand and introduced himself, "Hi, my name is John, you can call me Ace."

I felt silly calling him that, but my parents had trained me to respect authority and my elders. Ace was twenty-four. A vast gulf of three years separated us, the difference qualified him as my elder, and his newly minted flight instructor's rating established him as an authority.

Both new to this variant of the venerable Champ, we conducted a thorough preflight inspection. A good thing, too. Under the cowl we found the tiny engine had done more than make a lot of noise, it had also redesigned the cowling. The nasty little engine vibrated. A lot! It didn't just shake; it tried to revolve around the crankshaft axis in response to every power stroke and had chafed the ignition wires to shreds when the upper spark plugs punched a pair of holes in the fiberglass cowling.

I installed new wires and with a half round file and enlarged the holes already in the fiberglass so the plugs could move in and out of the cowling without harming them.

Inspection, modification, and repairs complete, Ace and I climbed in and took off. The climb required everything the little engine had, and a half hour to claw our way to the dizzy altitude of four thousand feet where Ace improvised a lesson in spins.

"Not just the wimpy spin recognition you learned to get a license; in this machine, we can do the real thing!" he screamed over the noise because headsets, ubiquitous now, were still in the future. "Hold the stick lightly, put your feet on the rudder pedals and follow me through."

Whatever.

Throttled back, the rush of wind replaced the roar of the miniature engine. The nose went up, the airspeed needle unwound and, quick as a slide projector, earth going 'round and 'round in the windshield replaced sky. After a couple of turns, he recovered, added power, and we struggled to climb back up so I could try.

Spin training was interesting, but not the reason for the checkout, so I yelled, "Ace, what's this have to do with learning to land this thing?"

"Nothing, take us back, and I'll show you how."

I thought so, he'd been avoiding the landing.

On final, instead of having me follow through, he shouted, "I'll crab into the wind and hold the upwind wing down so we don't drift. You watch."

Over the numbers, Ace made no attempt to correct the left crab before contact with the asphalt, and Newton's physics took charge. Bam, bounce, bam, screech, veer left, right brake to correct, too much, and the inevitable veer right was followed by an arc to the left when the wind pushed the tail.

We lurched to a stop in the center of the runway after the smoking tires had absorbed our momentum.

I was impressed and asked, "Is landing a taildragger always so exciting?"

"Yeah, that's pretty normal," he replied, unbuckled his seat belt, climbed out, then leaned back in and asked, "Think you have the hang of it?"

"Sure, that didn't seem so hard. You wanna get back in and ride to the office?"

"Nope, I'll walk, she's all yours."

The wily little Champ had other ideas. A newly minted tailwheel pilot, I taxied to the run-up pad and stopped the Champ's forward progress with a gentle application of the brakes like he taught me. Aggressive braking could put it on its nose. So far, so good.

I went through the run-up checklist. "Brakes set, stick back, trim set, seatbelt secure, door fastened, instruments set, fuel on," then pushed the throttle in to increase power for the mag check, and... nothing! Throttle in and throttle out had no effect on the noise.

Rats! The distant end of the cable isn't in communication with the carburetor and must be the latest victim of the vibration. There's still time to save this and get in a flight. I'll shut it down, push it back to the shop, fix it, and then go fly.

I pulled the mixture control to deprive the engine of fuel and got a cabin full of push/pull cable for my trouble.

Oh, crap, now what? Switch off the magnetos, kill the ignition.

By now, I'd become accustomed to disconnected controls in the worthless machine and wasn't surprised when the ignition switch had no effect.

Great, the mags are still hot, broken 'P' leads.

Even though the list of necessary repairs was long, she wasn't finished making sure I didn't fly. While I searched for the fuel shutoff, the airplane began an un-commanded pirouette to the left when the right brake pedal faded and became more pedal than brake. Curious, I looked outside in time to see a geyser of red brake fluid shoot up and carom off the bottom of the wing. Not content, the plane's left turn diminished with no input from me when that brake also disappeared. Two broken lines.

Dang! Where is that fuel valve?

With the brakes off the job, the Champ began to roll, and I employed my newly acquired skills to steer the airplane away from the runway where an encounter of the unpleasant kind waited, and into a field of tall grass instead. The airplane-come-threshing-machine harvested hay until the engine consumed the fuel that remained in the line after I found the shutoff.

In the silence that followed, a pleasant breeze blew propeller-cut grass through the open window, warm sunlight streamed in the windshield, the sweet odor of aircraft brake fluid filled my nostrils, and faraway laughter accompanied the metronomic ticking of the cooling engine.

Well, I'll be damned, nothing major is broken.

Although the slow-motion sashay into the weeds was embarrassing, it was the best outcome. To attempt a landing in the crosswind with no actual experience would have been a sure disaster. The classy little Champ knew better than to let me try.

A voice I must have imagined, but one that remains in memory as vivid as my mother's, broke the stillness.

"Mikie, come back after someone replaces my freak motor with a real airplane engine and we'll go flying together on a calm summer morning.

It'll be fun."

32. An example of the Champ that taught me a lesson.

Inspiration is a Complicated Thing

Seven thousand hours in the air, I land, and already anticipate the next flight.

Organic, sensuous like no manmade machine has a right to be, born of the cold light of aerodynamic law and immutable laws of physics.

Pure right brain, form follows function.

Yet, from the same place in a mind that appreciates a beautiful woman and falls in love, gray matter is intoxicated by the lines of the well-designed airplane.

Raw material, wood, aluminum, steel, cloth, rubber, and paint, assembled by skilled hands becomes sculpture, the frozen breath of the designer; pure emotional energy.

No airplane was ever called "He."

In flight, right brain veers left into three-dimensional life, gravity's law temporarily repealed.

Thrust defeats drag, compresses time-space to leap tall mountains in a single bound.

Aviators, human nature at its best, all welcome to enter through the 'Needle's Eye' of training on bended knee.

Anyone can buy in, some will have to beg; willing students of an unnatural art, only the humble survive.

Air, like the sea is not inherently dangerous, but terribly unforgiving of error.

Flight's elixir, the heady sweet odor of avgas, hot oil, hydraulic fluid, butyrate dope, and hot metal induce legal public intoxication.

Its music, the alto rattle of the rivet gun, an air-motor's soprano whine, the tenor hum of conversation, and bass drum grumble of a radial engine as it coughs to life, is accompanied by the percussion pop of a welding torch, triangle ring of a wrench, and laughter that pours from the concert hall of a Hangar.

Four when Mother folded a humble piece of paper and said, "Watch."

The slick dart floated across the basement and hit the wall, fwaaap. Hooked, the course of life was set.

Simple and uncomplicated inspiration.

Thank you, Mother for the paper plane, Irv for the lessons, and Dad for the books, models, and sharing your passion.

33. Mother's Magic

PART II

JAMES

12.

Run up to War

I knew little of Dad's childhood. He was born in Hollywood, California on December 6, 1926, the year after the invention of miniature golf and the same year PEZ candy was invented to cover smoker's breath.

"Like you, my older brothers and I loved the beach, but unlike the Oregon coast with its frigid water, we could dive for abalone in the warm ocean. I helped Ray and Bill haul home their catch in a burlap bag, and your grandma would make a delicious soup served with homemade bread. It was great.

"Oh yeah, the Mexican food here is fake. In our neighborhood, we had Mexicans with a pushcart who sold tamales wrapped in a corn husk, real Mexican food."

He never developed a taste for Taco Bell, and that was all I would learn from him about his childhood.

Grandma added her two bits to the idyllic life I imagined in magical Hollywood when she told me, "I loved the movies. We used to go to the lot and watch them being made. One day I read an ad in the paper; a studio needed kids to try out, so I took your dad to the audition. They were looking for a kid to play the role of Spanky in the *Our Gang* series. He got the part, but Grandpa Clarence squashed the deal. He didn't like the movies."

Although I never knew Clarence, who died in 1941, I think he was a pretty poor sport. Dad's skill as a thespian would eventually be put to the test on a stage of life or death.

Grandma continued, "We were rich; your grandpa was an inventor. He designed a thing called the 'dry channel system,' or something like that. It's a tool that men working on power lines used in the rain to keep them safe from being electrocuted, and still do today. Even though the Depression was in full swing, we had a lot of money, and Clarence bought me a really swanky car, a Stutz Black Hawk Speedster."

I suspect Grandma had no driver's license; she wrapped the Stutz around a phone pole and never drove again.

In a book by Perry Whiting, Clarence's first cousin, I discovered a backstory to this. After a life of poverty in Norfolk, Virginia, they were recent immigrants to California compliments of Perry, Clarence's generous, wealthy first cousin and well-known Los Angeles businessman.

Perry had significant real estate holdings, and I believe did much more than just relocate the family. According to the 1928 city directory, my recently broke grandparents owned a home at a time when local bankers could only afford to rent.

Perry likely financed the patent that made the money, as there's no employment information about Clarence in the city directory for a number of years. Perry must also have been well-respected by my grandparents if their choice of names says anything. It can be no coincidence my father's middle name was Henley, the name of the real estate company Perry used. They named a son Perry Whiting Dennis, and a second one also carried Whiting for a middle name.

In 1936 the money sky fell; something went wrong with the cash flow from the patent. When I asked Grandma about it, she mumbled what might have been a dirty word and said more clearly in her Virginia accent, "That damned crooked lawyer."

Corruption, the catalyst that provoked a move from California to Eatonville, Washington also forced Clarence to take whatever work he could find as an electrician with various small companies until he finally settled into an eighteen-month stint with the U.S. Army Signal Corps at Ft. Lewis.

1939, the year Germany attacked Poland and ignited World War II, the family moved again, this time west to Poulsbo, a village of fishermen and loggers that clung precariously to the slope above Liberty Bay on the Kitsap Peninsula, and my mother's ancestral home.

Twelve years old, new to the community, my father was three years older than Joyce Young, granddaughter of two of the town's founding fathers.

Although I never lived there, when anyone asked me where I came from, my internal compass pointed squarely at Poulsbo. From age two I had free run of the town, open credit at the drugstore soda fountain, and was certain Grandpa was the 'King of Poulsbo' which, of course, made me 'The Prince of Poulsbo.'

It's all about me.

By 1940, war loomed, and opportunity blossomed in the nearby Puget Sound Navy Shipyard where Clarence easily found employment.

Sunday, June 22, 1941, Germany shocked the world and invaded the Soviet Union.

After the slide from financial comfort into the maelstrom of the Depression, it must have been a relief for the family to feel secure in a well-paying government job until life dealt another cruel blow.

While at work on the heavy cruiser, U.S.S. New Orleans, September 3, 1941, age fifty-three, Clarence suffered a heart attack and fell dead on the spot.

There's no record to explain the why of what happened next, but a few days later, Grandma gathered up her youngest son Bob and boarded an eastbound train to her family home in Norfolk, Virginia.

34. Perry Whiting's book, "Experiences of a Pioneer"

Fourteen, two weeks into the ninth grade, my father remained behind, alone, a high school dropout.

It sounds bad in modern terms, but at the time, school beyond the eighth grade was a privilege, not a necessity; to care for family, the farm, or fight for your country, a badge of honor. For those who left school to answer the call of duty or family, the GI Bill and the GED would be created by a grateful nation.

Death and abandonment demanded self-sufficiency, and opportunity beckoned in Bremerton where the Navy shipyard expanded by sixty to seventy men a day. Too young to work in the yard, his immediate cash flow crisis was resolved by a menial job on the Black Ball Ferry that carried workers to and from Seattle. His share of twenty-nine boring trips a day was followed shortly by employment in the Merchant Marine.

Sea stories, like all his stories, were bereft of detail. Over time, I learned to ask him the same question again; I might learn some new information.

"What did you do in the Merchant Marine?"

"I told you, I was a cabin boy."

"I know, but what does that mean, exactly?"

"It was simple; do whatever anyone asked. Deliver a tray of coffee mugs across a pitching deck or, slippery lifeline in one hand, hammer in the other, I chipped ice from the ship or helped the engineers in the sweltering engine room. In time, I became the youngest 'rated fireman' in the Merchant navy."

Now we're talking, the youngest rated fireman!

Spellbound, I listened and imagined a swashbuckling life on the high seas. He didn't mention where they traveled or the name of the ship, and I never thought to find out. The only question I asked was, "How'd you get into the Merchant Marine when you were only fourteen?"

"I wondered when you'd figure that out. It's a story I'm not proud of," and another example of his ability to answer a question without providing enlightenment.

"Times were tough. Dad had died, Mom and Bob went to Virginia, I had a dead-end job as a porter on the Black Ball Ferry and, well, I screwed up and landed before the local judge who gave me a choice. 'Son, you can go to jail or, since you look big for your age, you can join the Merchant Marine.'"

How or why he ended up in front of the judge, never explained; he simply added, "I joined."

13.

Scars

Scars, Inside

Time passed, and the pattern of terrified shopkeepers continued until it finally occurred to me to ask, "When you were looking for Nazis in hiding, how did you find them, where would you look? Did the Army give you a book of pictures and say, 'Here's Fritz, go find him'? Europe is a big place."

He looked at me evenly for a moment, then instead of one of his answers that entertained but didn't enlighten, he surprised me.

"No, there was no book of pictures. I knew where to look, where they lived, who their friends were, and where they'd go in a crisis."

Master of the obvious, I responded, "How?"

"Some were my friends; others, just people I met."

More confused than ever, at a loss for words, again I stupidly asked, "How?"

"I can't tell you."

He's drifting away, got that faraway look, going into the odd place he won't return from for days.

Thirteen, and not always as careful with my mouth as I should have been, I taunted, "Why won't you talk? Are you afraid of Germans? We won."

Then the man I knew to be afraid of nothing shocked me when he snapped, "No, not Germans. I'm afraid of Americans, and if we keep talking, you'd need to be, too."

What are you talking about, you're afraid of Americans, and if they, whoever 'they' are, knew I knew, I'd have to be afraid, too? That's nuts, I live in the same house; 'they' must already assume I know.

I looked up and searched his face for insight but, eyes focused on infinity, he looked right through me and sightlessly stared into an unfathomable cauldron of horror invisible to me.

Damn! He's gone again.

Instinctively I knew we wouldn't be discussing this anymore and didn't, either, not for a long time.

Scars, Outside

July 1963, weeks after I'd pestered Dad about his reticence to talk about his war experience, my best friend Steve Polimeni came from Portland to visit our new home in eastern Oregon.

After a long day of play in the desert, Dad drove us, hot, sweaty, and dust-streaked the two miles to Radium Hot Springs swimming pool to cool off and, for Mother's benefit, clean up.

In the dressing room, while we changed from street clothes into swimming suits, Steve whispered, "What happened to your dad's back? It looks awful."

From the top of his neck to his heels, he looked like a pincushion. Thousands of small craters covered his skin.

"It happened after the war. He lived in Bruck, Germany. One night he and a friend walked home from a pub, and they heard something 'thump' on the road behind them. He told me, 'We guessed we'd been targeted by an angry local, and the thud sound, likely a hand grenade.'"

"What'd they do?"

"They ran."

"What happened?"

"The thing exploded and peppered him with steel slivers that sometimes work out, and Mom uses tweezers to remove them.

Now and then, he goes to the doctor who x-rays him to find the big ones and takes out enough to fill a pill bottle."

"Is that why his shoulder looks funny?"

"No, that's different, he's missing a bone there. He told me he was using an air hammer that exploded, and a piece hit him in the back and shattered his clavicle."

"How'd something in front of him hit him in the back?"

"I don't know."

"Why does he stand crooked?"

"He was in a car accident after he came home from the war and spent most of a year in a body cast."

"How'd that happen?"

"I'm not really sure. I think he fell asleep or something."

Although embarrassed by Steve's questions, the short attention span of new teens saved me when we exhausted everything of interest from the topic and jumped in the pool. I never said so, but the conversation haunted me and reminded me of my question.

'Are you afraid of Germans?'

His answer, *'No, I'm afraid of Americans,'* made no sense.

Could his injuries have something to do with the answer?

Too young to pursue the question, I never forgot it.

Adaptation

"Normal" is what you become accustomed to; at our house, German shopkeepers terrified of Father was normal, and in 1964, we added a new twist to it, a reoccurring nightmare.

When I returned home from wherever I'd been, I learned to look for the telltale flash of an ambulance parked in our front yard.

Alerted by the lights, I'd choke down fear's bile and, pulse pounding, run toward their unmistakable message of terror: another heart attack. Or worse.

We came to depend on the usual pattern for heart disease, a call for the ambulance followed by time in the hospital, recuperation at home, then back to work.

Ten years later, in 1974, Dad's recurring adventures with heart disease culminated in emergency surgery at a specialty clinic in Seattle, two hundred-fifty miles away, where he received a triple bypass, one of the first.

This trip would veer from normal in one significant way. He came home, but nerves damaged by the surgery caused him chronic pain in cool weather, and he started wearing his long wool overcoat on shirtsleeve days.

After recovery, he became a devotee of the coronary bypass, a spokesman for the American Heart Association, and traveled the world to lecture on the attributes of the new procedure. We encouraged him to slow down, but he assured us, "Don't worry, I'm good as new."

In an attempt to maintain my sense of normal, recovery after catastrophe, I naively accepted his story at face value.

Bypass surgery at forty-seven must mean he's good for forty-seven more.

Near Death as Truth Serum

To celebrate his recovery, I took him to the coast for his favorite activity, ocean salmon fishing. After three days of chasing the fish with a friend in his boat, I drove us home in the wee hours of the morning. Unprompted, cloaked in night's anonymity and possibly mellowed by his recent brush with death or the drugs they had him on, he began to talk.

"Mike, I know you're curious about my life before you. The stories I told you are true but incomplete. I wasn't part of the Jedburgh program; I was recruited for something a little different. I was offered big money to learn German and discovered why, later."

I thought so; there has to be more.

"How'd you learn so many dialects, so quickly?"

"Good question. I was sent to the Midwest to stay with a German-speaking family who wouldn't let me eat until I could say 'pass the potatoes' in perfect German. Starvation is a good motivator.

"The finishing school for language was at Fort Bragg. For the final exam, the instructors came into the barracks while we slept and tipped over our beds. Anyone who woke up swearing, in any language other than German, washed out.

"After language school, they sent me to a camp in Canada for specialized combat training."

I hear the double qualifier.

"Specialized combat training, what's that, and why Canada?"

I have a pretty good idea.

He wouldn't say where, but as time goes by and more information is declassified, the clues all point to one place.

Unofficially known as Camp X, Special Training School No. 103 established December 6, 1941, Dad's birthday, was the first secret agent training school built in North America. The camp was developed by British S.O.E., now MI6, for the sole purpose of linking Britain and the United States in spite of an act of Congress that forbade U.S. involvement in the war.

The camp was at a remote location on the shores of Lake Ontario, yet only thirty miles straight across the lake from the U.S. and only five miles from D.I.L., the largest armaments manufacturing facility in North America.

U.S. president Franklin D. Roosevelt chose William "Wild Bill" Donovan to be his "Coordinator of Information", a position that was soon to become the nation's spy service, the Office of Strategic Services, O.S.S., and later, the C.I.A.

Donovan was keen to develop a cadre of secret agents, and Camp X was designed to help. The camp's sole purpose, over a ten-week period, to train recruits from around the world, including Americans, in every aspect of silent killing, unarmed combat, sabotage, demolition, map reading, weaponry, and Morse Code.

A spy, by definition, lives outside of the protections of the Geneva Convention and therefore his training would also be unconventional. The life or death nature of the work is exemplified by the following excerpt from the training manual.

5. Searching a prisoner, if you are armed... Kill him first. If that is inconvenient, make him lie face to the ground, hands out in front. Knock him out with a rifle butt, side or butt of a pistol or your boot. Then search him.

35. Aerial view of Camp X

A career as a spy was an iffy thing; five percent success in the field was considered worth the effort by the high command.

"In England, the British S.O.E. decided, because of my age, language skill, and special training, I'd go to Germany."

"Germany? Why, what for?" I blurted. No longer a child smitten by the idea of adventure, I added, "So, you were a spy?"

"Yes, of sorts."

"What sort?" I asked, expecting a story of secret radio transmitters, maps printed on silk, a miniature button compass, life on the lam in enemy territory, and unprepared for his answer.

"I was just a kid, seventeen, too young to serve in anyone's army when the French underground smuggled me into Berlin, where I lived in the home of a baker and his family. The baker, an anti-Nazi spy, passed me off as a refugee cousin.

"Hitler had a sweet tooth and a standing order of pastry for his Army Headquarters. Every morning, I delivered the order, hung out a while, talked, listened, and reported back what I'd heard."

"Weren't you afraid?"

"Naw, who doesn't love the doughnut boy? I made a lot of friends."

For once I kept my mouth shut and waited out the silence that followed.

He continued, "In late 1944, the 8th Air Force was relentlessly bombing Berlin by day. The RAF dropped bombs at night, and a decision was made to pull me out.

"In the entire history of German warfare, they'd never mounted an attack in December, choosing instead to fight when the weather is better.

"Again, tasked with my exfiltration, the French underground came and got me with orders to turn me over to the Allies in Belgium. The plan went like clockwork until we ran smack into the back of a surprise German offensive forever known as 'The Battle of the Bulge.'"

"Okay, let me get this straight, you were at the Battle of the Bulge, only on the wrong side of the lines?"

"Yuup. Scared to death, we hid in a barn."

"How old were you?"

"Juss turnn'd eighteeeen," he slurred.

I glanced at him, but he'd fallen asleep. I drove through the night and thought about what he'd said.

Although the story had little of the nail-biting trauma of battle, it had its own devastating stress. An American kid in Germany, without uniform or military affiliation, would be continuously subjected to the stress of a known outcome should he be caught.

Summary execution; death by hanging with piano wire.

14.

A New Direction

Ring, ring, ring... "Hello."

"Hey there, Mike, what are you doing? Still working for the railroad? I've got a great idea. We need to talk."

Dad wasn't really interested in what I was doing.

He knows I'm not working for the railroad I hate, but he's got an idea, and I'm pretty sure he wants me to make it happen.

"Remember, the railroad let me go when the foot I injured didn't heal? I'm working at the airport with a full-length cast on my leg."

"How much are they paying you? Why don't you move here? We can be partners in my idea; I'm sure you can do much better here."

Hmmmmm... He's right, as usual. As much as I love airplanes, the business doesn't love me back, and I'm using small bits of the injury settlement to subsidize my income, but he also hasn't talked money.

"Okay, let's hear it."

That's how we came to move from Portland back to Walla Walla. In his garage, I sorted out the how of his idea to remanufacture irrigation sprinklers that wore out prematurely when the big corporate farms reclaimed desert by pumping millions of gallons of silt-laden water directly from the Columbia River onto tens of thousands of acres of newly planted potatoes.

Two guys, Pete and George, were converting miles of desert into farmland. People called it 'Pete and George's folly.' Everyone was surprised, even Pete and George, when the first crop came out of the fertile but previously dry ground at not the norm, ten tons to the acre, but sixty, and paid off the multimillion-dollar project in the first year.

Before the celebrating was over, the sprinklers that made the miracle happen began to fly off the irrigation pivots. Sprinklers that previously had clear well water pumped through them and lasted twenty years now fell off the pipe in one season, ruined by the gritty river water.

Dad watched this happening and correctly surmised there would be a market for a service that could remanufacture the sprinklers for less cost than new ones.

My job, develop the machines and processes to make new sprinklers from old. Quickly.

He would do what he did best, talk and knock on doors to sell the farmer/manager on his concept of annual refurbishment.

Promoting a new and untried concept is a daunting task, but as usual, he had a plan.

Sprinklers essential for the efficient cultivation of vast tracts of dry land didn't just spray water, they also delivered herbicide and fertilizer.

Giant pivots a quarter-mile long, new computer-controlled technology, a pipe on wheels with sprinklers along its length turned like the hand of a clock. A jammed sprinkler that failed to turn properly, impossible to detect by eye, ruined many acres of potatoes as the big machine made its way around the field.

Always ahead of the curve, Dad knew of and bought the brand-new NASA Landsat satellite pictures of the farms he intended to visit. In their living rooms, he'd show the farmer how a damaged sprinkler destroyed his crop. Potatoes were one shade of gray in the thermal images; pigweed, another. While standing in the mud beside the field a half-mile wide, they looked exactly alike.

"See that," he pointed at the round smear in the picture of a specific pivot. "That's pigweed, and there's no spuds under it. We can refurbish your sprinkler heads for half the price of a new one. Crate 'em up, send 'em to us in winter, we'll get 'em back before spring."

He signed them up in minutes.

Success was still in the future that first winter when my first wife and I lived with our daughter in my parents' house. Two families under one roof don't cohabit well. In spite of the snow, twenty below temperatures, and no real job, we went house shopping with a local realtor, Doug.

"I know there are no houses on the market due to the cold weather, but we like old craftsman style homes. Will you show us a few until you get a feel for what we want?" I asked.

"Well, okay, I can do that, but don't get your hopes up until spring."

After we looked at several, Doug said, "I think I've got it. I'll take you by a house that's exactly what you have in mind, although it's not for sale. It belongs to my friend who sold it after thirty years, moved to the suburbs, hated it there, then bought the house back at a premium. They'll never move."

He was right, of course; the house was perfect.

"Thanks for the tour. We'll look forward to hearing from you," I told Doug. As we drove away, a windblown whiteout obscured the real estate office.

Three days later, he called. "I've got two houses to show you."

When we turned down the first one, Doug said, "I didn't think you'd like this one, but I had to show it to you first. You'll like the next one better."

Again, he was right when he drove us back to the "perfect house" from days before.

"This is for sale? I thought you said they'd never move."

"Yup, that's what I said, but Bill called my secretary this morning and told her they're moving to Boise to be closer to their grandchildren and are going to list the house."

"We'll take it."

Like that, a flash of magic, our perfect house was mysteriously for sale. Without a job, it was going to take more than magic to finance it. It was gonna require a miracle.

The next day at the Savings and Loan, I sat with Steve the loan officer, smiled, and confidently told him, "I have twenty-five percent of the price for a down payment."

"I see that, and that's nice, but you didn't fill in the employment part. Do you have a job?"

"I know it sounds goofy, but well, sorta," I answered and explained the new business venture.

"So, no, you don't have a job. I can't take this application to the loan committee."

"Yes, you can."

"They'll turn it down for sure."

"Maybe, but you take it to them and let them turn it down."

Reluctantly, he agreed, "I'll call you on Wednesday after the meeting."

I can read the tea leaves. I don't have a chance in Hell.

"Great, see you then."

Steve called Wednesday morning. Incredulity dripped from the phone when he said, "If you have the time today, I have the mortgage papers ready to sign."

"We'll be right there," I answered then rushed to the office before someone came to their senses.

"Who are you?" he asked.

"No one, why?"

"As I thought, the committee turned down your application in seconds. Just before the meeting ended, the president of the bank shocked everyone when he asked me, 'That loan we turned down for the Dennis', are they related to Jim Dennis?'

"'Yes, he's Mike's father.'

"'Oh, in that case, approve the loan.'"

No idea why that happened, I beat a hasty retreat before the bubble of good fortune could burst.

I told Dad what had happened and asked why.

He gazed off into the distance a moment, then answered, "This community can mistreat a banker whose wife has a problem with addiction. I worked with her on the sly for a couple of years to get her unhooked."

Understanding, compassion for addiction, and the Betty Ford Clinic were far in the future.

While the business matured, and sprinklers were in use during summer, to pay the mortgage I subsidized my meager salary with airplane maintenance.

PME, Product Marketing Enterprises, grew from a repair concept to one of remanufacturing by replacing worn parts with all new components manufactured on the premises. Over a five-year run, I developed the equipment to efficiently dismantle, repair, reassemble, and test sprinklers. When it became apparent that making new parts was more efficient than repairing old ones, I became adept at either designing and building custom machines or modifying conventional equipment to make coil springs, parts made from turned brass, aluminum, stainless steel, rubber, and plastic. Complex cast bronze components were made with the 'lost wax' process.

The hundreds of long strips of material that remained when I cut round plastic washers from them littered the production floor and made Dad crazy.

"There must be something they're good for," he said as he wrapped a strip around his head.

I'd developed the dies that replaced a twenty-five-cent part with one that cost two-tenths of a cent. His thrift made me crazy, so I installed a trim knife on the press and clipped the strips into little squares with a hole in the middle that fell into a small trash can.

"What are those?" he asked as he peered into the trash can.

"The waste from the washers."

"Oh."

As intended, he lost interest and quit pestering me. A good thing for both of us.

I knew he felt he still had much to do, and, as it turned out, little time to get it done.

Many Hats

A church pastor, chaplain at the VA hospital, director of Prison Industries, court appointed counselor for the wealthy and connected, partner with me in a manufacturing concern, and two kids still at home, he had one more thing to take care of.

What to do for the community of people who fell through the cracks, the people trapped in alcoholic addiction from our end of the economic spectrum. People he called, "My people."

First, he established an Alcoholics Anonymous group that met in our house until Mother got her fill of cigarette smoke and cleaning up the debris of stale coffee and cigarette butts.

His solution, quietly raise money to buy what he called a "halfway house," a large home where people with addiction issues and nowhere to go could live if they participated in a recovery program. Until he could hire a manager, he was the director.

When he needed something, he invited me to breakfast at his favorite beanery. "Mike, I've got an idea."

Uh, oh.

"Some of the guys at the house are at the point where they need and can hold down a job. You need people to work at the shop; this could work out for everyone."

Oh, boy, there it is, my contribution to his vision. How can I say no?

"What do you need, Dad?"

"That's the spirit! I'll sober them up, and you hire them. It'll be great for everyone!"

I have to appreciate his optimism, but 'great' might be overstating it.

"What do you want to do first?"

"Hire Harvey."

Harvey, good choice. I like him.

36. Dad and me, Walla Walla, WA

"Okay."

For a few weeks, the scheme worked well, until one morning Harvey tried to rope me into a modification.

"See this? It's my Antabuse; I have to take one of these every day. They make me allergic to alcohol so I get sick if I drink. I'm gonna put the pill bottle up here on the shelf, and you can make sure I take one every day."

Whoa, whoa, whoa, hold your horses, pal.

"No, Harvey, I don't think so. Take the pills home. They're your responsibility, not mine."

"Oh, okay. It seemed like a good idea."

I bet it did. Make me responsible for you taking the pill and the next time you go on a bender, it's my fault.

I liked him, but when he disappeared only to reappear days later on my front porch at midnight, he forced me to provide the rejection he craved.

"Miiike, hiiii, ish me Harvey, I know, you know, I'm druuunk, hell, I knows I'm druunk, toooo."

Irrefutable logic.

"I beeeeen druuunk'n the hard stuff an' need ta come down easy-like. Yous can gets me a jug of wines so's I can comes down easy-like, and I cans shtay in your bashment for a few days. Whatcha think?"

I was afraid of this. No, is what I think.

"Harvey, you know I like you; no, I can't do that. I'll call the 'house' and get someone to come over here and get you."

"Yeah, I thunk so... no don't calls, I cants go thresh."

He went back to his truck, started it, ground the gears, and wove into the night.

I never saw him again.

Please Dad, no more, this is too painful.

After Dad surprised everyone and moved the family to Hawaii, I was left with his original partner. Without Dad to leaven the relationship, he and I didn't get along. In time, I eliminated the stress for us both and sold him my share to pursue a life in the airplane business.

Before it closed forty years later after farm technology changed and abandoned impact sprinklers, PME, the only business of its kind, remanufactured millions of them.

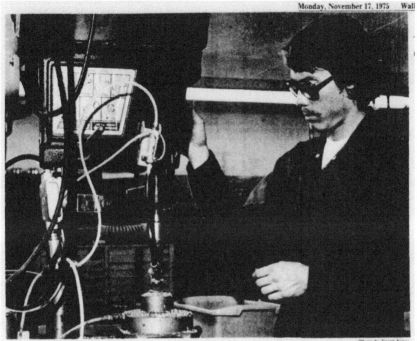

Monday, November 17, 1975   Wall

(Photo by Frank King)

Bob Freeman drills out old parts in preparation to assembling the rebuilt sprinkler head

37. Image and article from Nov 17, 1975 Walla Walla Union-Bulletin

Sprinkler-head repair shop grows from family operation

Product Marketing Enterprises, Inc. is a Walla Walla Industry which has slowly emerged from a family operation in a garage to an enlarged shop and office at 1011 N. 9th Ave. PME is an irrigation sprinkler head rebuilding business started four years ago in the garage of Rev. James Dennis. It is now a two-family, nine employee operation. Principals in the firm are Dean Culbertson, Prescott wheat rancher, president; Dennis, a chaplain at the Veterans Administration Hospital here; and Michael Dennis, son of Rev. Dennis who is plant manager and a talented machinist. Betty Culbertson (Mrs. Dean) is the office secretary.

The idea for establishing a sprinkler head rebuilding business was jointly developed by the two Dennises and Culbertson. In the last four years they have rebuilt sprinklers for 1,500 customers in 11 western states. "I have heard of companies that repair sprinkler heads," Dennis said, "but as far as I know, we are the only one that completely rebuilds them with custom-manufactured parts."

When an order comes into the plant, the heads are completely disassembled. Old bushings and washers are removed with special tools, Dennis said. The reusable parts are cleaned and reassembled. Each unit receives new rocker pins and springs, new brass riser bearing bushings, new spindles if necessary, brass bushings in the rocker arms and a PME long-life washer package is installed. After assembly, each head is pressure-tested in the shop before it is returned to the customer.

PME started by using factory-built parts for their rebuilding process but went to manufacturing their own due to higher costs and inability of manufacturers to supply parts. "We developed our own replacement parts and now manufacture our own washer package, bend our own springs and machine bushings of brass and pins from stainless steel," Dennis said. There are three field representatives working for PME, two in the Washington-Oregon area and one in Twin Falls, Idaho.

"Junked sprinklers not operating or not performing properly can only cost the farmer money," according to Culbertson. "Many irrigators have gone into a systematic rebuilding program. A third, or even half, of their total units are sent in to us each year for rebuilding."

"Having Dean with us is probably why we are so successful in offering a good marketable product," Dennis said. "He looks at everything from the farmer's point of view, including service and price." PME claims it can completely rebuild a sprinkler head for about half what it costs for a new one. PME has grown from a one-man operation in a garage to a healthy small business in four years.

"We hope to grow even more rapidly in the coming four years," Dennis said.

38. "Group therapy at Half Way House". *Image and article from Aug. 29, 1971 Walla Walla Union-Bulletin*

New House 'Half Way House' For Treatment of Alcoholics

New House is a half-way house, a recovery facility for alcoholics. The center was established in mid-June and has been operating ever since in the Marcus House, the student center of the First Congregational Church. The house was established to provide treatment, living facilities and a therapeutic environment for recovering men alcoholics. Since the beginning of the half-way house from five to ten men have been in continuous residence. The Rev. James Dennis, chaplain of the Veterans Administration Hospital, is the temporary executive chairman, and serves with a small executive committee that administers the new organization.

Rev. Dennis said, "The house was established so we can provide aid, counseling, and treatment to men who want to quit drinking. We have set up a counseling program and each one of the men is undergoing individual and group therapy. We have available to us psychologists, physicians, and lay analysts that help us in this phase. In addition, the men regularly attend local meetings of Alcoholics Anonymous."

In addition to the therapy sessions, living in this type of environment aids the recovering alcoholic. He is with men who are encountering many of the same type of problems he has. He has a clean place to live, good food, and a home-like atmosphere. This environment seems to help in recovery for alcoholics, because it is not sterile, institutionalized and impersonal, and it is a lot better than a lonely hotel room. The men pay $25 per week for their food and lodging. Most of them are employed, but some are on some type of public assistance. There is no paid staff for New House. All of the work is done by professional and lay volunteers. Rev. Dennis is the temporary chairman of the organization formed to administer operation of the house. He is assisted by Dr. Michael Crow, Bill Reitz, and Earl Sherry. Dennis, Reitz, and Crow are all on the staff at the Veterans Administration Hospital and are heavily involved in alcoholism work.

Through the efforts of the Rev. Emrys P. Thomas, pastor of the First Congregational Church, the Marcus House was made available for the half-way house. It can be used as such until the middle of September. A special committee has been formed to look for new quarters for New House and negotiations are currently underway for a large home close to the downtown area of Walla Walla. Those on the real estate committee locating the new facility are John Wylie, Don Patch, and Harold Hanson. The New House temporary advisory board approved the acquisition of new quarters. As soon as negotiations are finalized, the location of New House will be announced.

Since New House started operation, many individuals and organizations have donated supplies and materials. The house has obtained beds and bedding, dishes, and cooking utensils. When the move is made to the new home there will be a need for furniture, rugs, and incidental household effects. The board will probably be staging a drive in the near future to furnish the new facility. All individuals, or organizations, wishing to contribute furnishings or materials should contact the Alcoholism and Referral Center in the Denny Building. New House is well along in forming a non-profit corporation to administer the organization. The articles of incorporation are expected to be signed in the near future and a board of directors and officers named.

There are five recovery houses such as New House situated in different cities in Washington. Some, like Sundown M Ranch near Yakima, have intensive, highly developed therapy programs. Others, the smaller half-way houses such as New House, work with what resources there are in the community in helping the recovering alcoholic. These treatment centers provide an important link in the chain of recovery for many alcoholics. Many alcoholics have lost their job, homes and families. New House is a place for them to start over, on the long road to recovery. Rev. Dennis said, "So far we have accomplished a lot in a short time. We have done so well because so many worked so hard. If we keep on as well we can become a self-supporting institution. It would be good if we could keep it this way without any type of governmental support. We should look at New House as a form of investment."

For every alcoholic in the United States it is estimated that he directly or indirectly affects the lives of six other individuals. There are over 9 million alcoholics in the United States. 758,000 of them are in Washington. The Washington State Department of Health estimates that there are 300 alcoholics, both men and women, in Walla Walla. "Anything we can do to cut down on this terrible waste of human resources is a plus sign on the ledger," Dennis said. "When an alcoholic is returned to society and productive living it is a return on a human investment in addition to eliminating a drain on public funds and resources."

How successful is New House in helping the recovered alcoholic? This isn't known as yet and only evaluation, research, and case following will be able to shed light on chances of recovery. This much is known though. In facilities such as Sundown M Ranch, men alcoholics who return to society, to jobs and families, have a good chance of making it. Over half of them never take another drink again and remain sober all their lives.

15.

Exit

A vacation in Hawaii brought Dad complete relief from the nerve damage, but his distress returned as soon as he came back to winter at home. Two weeks later he flew back to Hawaii to speak at a conference and, once again, the pain subsided.

He called Mother and said, "Sell the house, pack up the stuff, and ship it to Maui. I've rented us a place, and I'm the new chaplain at the prison. You'll love it here."

Irked at being saddled with the logistics of the move, she packed up, put the house on the market, moved the stuff, and didn't.

Like it on Maui, that is.

Ever able to make the worst of a good situation, she called the island, "The Rock," a thinly disguised reference to Alcatraz.

Protégé

Years before he left for Hawaii, Dad met and befriended Ben Vegors, a local pastor who had a deteriorating relationship with a congregation interested in a different direction.

In a video interview decades later, Ben, at the time ninety-five years old, described their relationship. "Jim asked me, 'Why don't you come out and volunteer at the Veterans Administration Hospital where I'm the chaplain? Since my heart surgery, I need help; someone to be on call at night and weekends.'

39. Dad in his office at the VA Hospital

"Jim became my mentor and friend. I didn't know it then, but he knew he was going to have to leave, and if I volunteered it would work into a full-time position.

"I came to love him. He was the most extraordinary man I ever met. He didn't know a stranger; give him ten minutes with a phone pole, and he'd strike up a lively conversation.

"I still miss him."

Ben Vegors was the oldest, longest-serving chaplain in the history of the VA.

Paradise

Dad wanted us to come to Hawaii and often said, "I want to share my island with you. You'd love it."

I didn't have the resources to take my family on the trip. Honestly, as well as broke, I felt abandoned and a little sorry for myself, stuck with a disagreeable business partner.

Three years later, June 1977, he called.

"I'd like to come visit. Can I stay with you guys?"

"Absolutely."

I'm surprised you feel the need to ask.

The visit didn't go as I expected.

On a mission, distracted, he had little to say and used our home as a base camp for a few days while he looked up every friend he had in the area, then flew to California and did the same there with people I didn't know.

As usual, on returning, he offered no explanation.

Mission accomplished, I drove him to the airport early in the morning on a Friday, tried to sit with him to wait for the plane, but he insisted, "Don't stay, you need to get to work; people are waiting for you," and hustled me out the door.

No one is waiting for me. You know the airplane business I left PME for fell apart and now I operate a one-man machine shop.

Outside the glass doors, I turned to watch him rummage through his briefcase.

Why do you always do that, hold me at arm's length?

I almost went back in but, intimidated by his insistence, didn't.

I wish I had.

I never saw him again.

40. In less than three years, Dad left his mark on Hawaii

16.

Circles Eventually Close

Nineteen, just days before I was to be unhappily married, he offered something rare, advice, but in his indirect way. "You do know, don't you, you don't have to go through with this?"

I have no idea what you're talking about, of course, I do; you taught me to keep my commitments.

I don't think I even nodded.

Fifteen years of misery followed until she abandoned her family and left.

Jude, my new wife who defined what a marriage should look like, got out of the plane we'd spent weeks traveling in and announced, "Flying is fun, but the pain from the headset is unbearable. You fix stuff for everyone else; will you fix that for me?"

Nice! She likes to fly, but the message is clear, all I have to do is fix the headset and I get to keep the plane.

Not only did I fix her complaint, but other people, when they tried her headset, asked for the same thing, and a hobby was born. One fix led to another.

I sat across the desk from the commander of the 123rd Fighter

Squadron, the oldest unit in the Oregon Air National Guard who'd begun with P-51's and now flew F-15 Eagles.

"Tom here showed me your new ear-seal design for a flight helmet. I like it. Are you going to make them?"

"No, sir, I can't. I need a custom made sewing machine. I have three kids and can't afford the machine."

"How much does it cost?"

"Ten thousand dollars, Sir."

In 1990 dollars, no less.

"Hmmmm." He drew a notepad from across his desk, wrote a few words, and handed it to me. "Will this help?"

Under the seal of the Air National Guard, the note read simply, "The Oregon National Guard is ordering $100,000 worth of headset ear-seals." His signature was scrawled across the bottom.

"Yes, Sir!"

As quickly as that, I ruined a perfectly good hobby and turned it into a business about to celebrate its third decade.

I know, what does that have to do with my dead father?

Fifteen years after I began, my mother said to me, "It's so nice to see you completed your dad's work. He'd be proud."

"What are you talking about?"

"He was in the hearing aid business."

"I know. So what?"

"Fighter pilot helmets is what. Remember the helmets he had in Portland, the ones you used to sneak out of the house and wear while you rode your bike around the block?"

She knew?

"Yes."

"Do you know what he was doing with them?"

"No."

"He was working with our neighbor, a fighter pilot who flew F-89 Scorpions, to design an ear-seal that didn't hurt and did a better job of protecting the pilot's hearing, but he failed. The materials of the time were inadequate. Now, you've finished his work."

This is too spooky; I have to ask.

"For who?"

"Why, the 123rd Fighter Squadron at the Air National Guard, is who. Same as you."

41. F-89 Scorpion

17.

One Last Adventure Together

Bob turned and walked toward his North American P-51 Mustang. As directed, I got up from the bench where he'd found me and followed him to close another circle that had begun a lifetime ago. Confronted with the reality of a childhood dream, about to fly a P-51, I stood in front of the airplane, mesmerized. His instruction came from far away.

"Steeep ooon the wheeeeel heeeere. Put yourrr ooother fooooot theeeeere. Staaaand wiiith booooth feeeeet on the wingggg walkkkk. Noooow, juuuust swinggg a leg overrrr the side ontooo the back seeeeat thennn swingggg the other one innnn and siiitt dowwwwn."

I climbed over the side and noticed there were no scratches in the green zinc chromate paint of the cockpit, and unwilling to leave the first, I moved at the speed of melting ice. Finally settled in the jump seat I'd designed for the back, I took a minute to observe the detail I knew so well from hours immersed in "The Book." Bob stood patiently on the wing, grinned and said, "How ya do'n there, sport," then leaned over and fastened the seatbelt I'd forgotten.

The P-51 is a single place fighter, and the jump seat behind Bob is where the bulky nineteen-forties era radios, a fuel tank, and armor plate had been. From the shallow cavern, I marveled at how relaxed he was as he swung first one, then the other leg over the cockpit coaming and slid into the new pilot-seat cushion I knew was there but couldn't see. I watched as he put on his gray helmet, plugged in the communication jacks, and fastened the double aerobatic harness. The snap of the master switch brought the intercom to life, a click in my headphones, and I heard the smile in his voice when he said, "Nice seat."

Calm as Joe Cool, I pushed the red intercom button. "Roger that." The eight-year-old, who still lives in a secret place in my head, appeared and was deliriously happy, proud to be part of, not just strapped into "The Pinnacle." I expected a visit from the kid, but he surprised me when he showed up with his thirty-one-year-old, immature, sometimes fun as hell, not-yet-dead at fifty, friend, Dad.

Dad used to come visit in dreams. I hadn't seen him in years, but he wasn't about to be left out of this adventure. The kid, Dad, me, and the P-51, together, felt just right. All crammed in the little back seat, we had plenty of room; the two extra crewmen only occupied space in my head. I didn't think we had a weight and balance problem, so I didn't distract Bob with the change in the passenger manifest. He was busy getting the thing going.

Switches on. Prop, fine pitch. Mixture rich. Throttle cracked. Fuel pump on. Bob shouted, "CLEAR!" The starter sang its whining alto howl and the huge, geared down four-blade propeller began to turn. Three or four blades passed when I heard the click of the mag switch turned to 'on'. Blam, blam chuff, puff, the spiral flow of the propeller captured the smoke of ignition, and the odor of hot exhaust twisted around the fuselage, through the open canopy, and up my nose.

Ambrosia!

Pop! Pop, pop, pop. Blam! Blam, blam, blam. Crackle, pop, crackle, crackle, pop, crackle. ROAR! The individual propeller blades dissolved into a shimmering disc, Bob closed the canopy, and a strangely familiar, non-aviation sound filled the cockpit. Surrounded by new sights and sounds, the steady chug a, chug a, chug a, chug sound of the Rolls-Royce V-12 engine surprised me. What happened to the lilting sound from outside, the lovely Doppler shift from twelve short, unmuffled stacks?

Inside, the sound was unlike any airplane I knew, a steady throbbing, a familiar chug a, chug a, chug a, chug a...

How do I know this sound?...

Oh! Sure, neurons finally connected the dots, there it was; a sound from another life, one far removed from aviation. A life so remote, so disconnected from my public passion for aviation, I'd been embarrassed to mention it to anyone who knew me.

In hindsight, my hated, almost-accidental employment as a railroad brakeman after my beloved world of aviation had collapsed into an economic recession was nothing to be embarrassed about. I was feeding my family but miserable doing it, dying by inches every day removed from my heart's desire.

The inside of a P-51 sounds just like the engine room of a diesel-electric locomotive. To be exact, a General Motors EMD FL9 "A" unit, popularly known as a "Streamliner." I spent two years in that purgatory of noise, fatigue, dirt, cold, heat, boredom, danger and, too full of unattractive self-pity to notice, adventure.

Twenty years old, I was insanely angry when my in-laws heard I finally had a 'real' job and gushed, "Oh, how wonderful. They have a great retirement plan. You were going to kill yourself in those 'little' airplanes."

Little did they know, in the late sixties, railroading was a life of danger so frequent, sudden, and spectacular, it made a busy life with airplanes seem almost risk-free. The men I worked with sixteen hours a day, no overtime, on average lost two families to divorce, retired at seventy-three and collected three retirement checks before they died. If they didn't get killed first. I had my own experiences with railroading danger.

Rearranged

What the hell is going on?

Pinned tight to the ceiling of the formerly stationary engine cab, the exquisite quality of the personal threat hasn't registered. A stranger in a once familiar land, I am fascinated by my rearranged world.

The screw top to my Thermos floats through the open window where the highway traffic is upside down. I've lost my appetite, and my sandwich. No longer in my hand, its constituent parts float in midair; vegetables, cheese, ham, two slices of bread, and a blob of mustard.

Interesting.

Like everything else in the cab, gravity has lost its grip on the blue milk crate I had my feet on a second ago. It's sliding up the windshield while my steel Thermos spins its cargo of iced tea into a golden nebula surrounded by a constellation of cigarette butts and dirt.

That's gonna make a mess.

It does, but not nearly as spectacular as the one outside. Five railcars and their contents are now in the middle of the highway.

We'd been waiting to reposition three 330,000-pound Alco Century Series engines while a Vancouver transfer going the other way set a cut of cars onto the track beside us.

A track gang protected themselves by aligning a switch into the siding where we sat, and the transfer slammed into us from behind. Nearly a million pounds of locomotives were instantly launched several hundred feet.

After the dust settles, the engineer and I pick ourselves up and climb from the cab.

Would you look at that! All three units are still on the rails.

We drive ourselves to the hospital where they x-ray us, pronounce us fit, and let us go.

It's a different time.

The Tyranny of Time

Everyone carries a railroad-approved pocket watch, train orders start and stop at a precise time, trains meet, arrive and depart on time, our lives are controlled by time, and as often as not, depend on it.

Four powerful road engines with a lightweight train of seventy-eight high-value merchandise cars wait at a red block signal.

Losing time.

The crew is confused. They have "rights" over every other train including passenger trains.

Why is this block red?

In fifteen seconds, those who survive will find out.

It's a revolutionary idea, well maybe only evolutionary, but it's novel. Since 1908, train crews of the Spokane Portland and Seattle Railroad have looped the route from Vancouver, Washington to Wishram, Washington, and back. A new crew based in Wishram will take the train further either east or south down the Oregon Trunk.

A new type of train, my train, is making the trip from Vancouver to Bend and skipping the crew change in Wishram. The new management is trying to sell shippers on the idea of a "fast freight" priority merchandise train to California. Half the normal complement of cars and twice the power. An overpowered, high-speed train capable of eating time.

I bid the job and got it with my useless low seniority number.

I don't know how, but I'll find out.

A normal freight departure is often hours behind schedule; this train is sitting in front of the depot, ready for us to get on and go!

On time!

Wow!

Only three notches of throttle and this thing flies, eighty miles an hour where we can, the fastest train on our line.

Only one set of rails on this line so inferior trains must take a siding and get out of the way. On time.

It's a dream job, get on, enjoy the ride, wave and smile at the train crews in the sidings as we blow by them with more power than two trains pulling half the weight. I've worked a few passenger trains; this is better and faster.

Five hours to Bend, Oregon, wait a while, catch the matching "fast freight" in the opposite direction; home in less than sixteen hours, a standard maximum duty day. Because we travel over what is normally four segments, we receive four days' pay.

Wow!

It's too good to last.

I have the job because it's the middle of winter. The guys with seniority had worked the Oregon Trunk in the winter with its cold and snow.

Historically, a run to Bend would include stopping to either remove or place a rail car at a number of businesses along the way. Waist deep snow, penetrating, dry, bone-chilling cold, a job for newbies.

"No, thanks."

Until they find out it's a 'milk run.' This train doesn't stop. We sit, warm and cozy in the engine where heaters blow all the hot air we need, and the caboose crew is warmed by a roaring oil stove.

Fifteen minutes before I'm to leave home to drive to my dream train, "Crusty," the board clerk, calls me to tell me I've been bumped.

Rats! Someone with more seniority has taken my job.

Crusty sends me to a job on the afternoon Willbridge switch engine to work with my least favorite conductor.

Purgatory for a day.

When I arrive home, the television is on and the news guy is talking about the horrible accident on the Oregon Trunk. Behind him are pictures of flaming wreckage, rail cars and engines twisted into grotesque shapes. Millions of pounds of equipment thrown about like children's toys.

Several fire engines spray water on the smoldering chaos as somber men peer into the crater where the train and tracks had been.

The block signal had been red because a cut of cars rolled out of the downhill sloped Bend Yard, jumped an ineffective derail onto the main line and quickly accelerated down the constant slope.

We are told kids released the cars.

Who knows?

Unnoticed, the cars rolled downhill through several towns on a sleepy Sunday night, and with no warning came around a corner and hit the stationary train at an estimated one-hundred-fifteen miles per hour.

The devastation was complete; the first two units were totally destroyed, killing the engineer and the fireman. The head brakeman, my position, was asleep in the third unit and injured so badly he never worked again. The swing brakeman and conductor in the caboose were also severely injured.

Fickle time, fifteen minutes between life and death.

The double funeral began on time.

At the End of the Taxiway

We stopped and set the brakes for the run-up; power up, check each mag and cycle the propeller. Strange, since starting the engine, the sound inside the aircraft hadn't changed. High power, low power, the same chug a, chug a. Interesting. I was sure it would change on takeoff. It didn't. Chug a, chug a, chug a, chug a, chug a... like a locomotive. I idly wondered how many people had the diversity of experience to homogenize the sound of those very different activities, railroading and aviation. I could, and suddenly appreciated them both more for it.

That was the first time I'd had anything good to say or even think about railroading. A ride in the pinnacle of piston-powered aviation perfection began a process that would salvage two lost years. The iconic airplane helped me reevaluate time I thought wasted, life miraculously salvaged from the trash heap of anger, full of valuable lessons, adventures, and stories.

Lined up on the runway, the souped-up race engine with three thousand horsepower accelerated the small fighter like a missile.

Rotate, positive rate, gear up, one big clunk/thud, a second big clunk/thud, the main gear and doors were up and closed, then two far-away, tiny little clunks when the tailwheel found its way home and politely shut the door behind itself.

Ten thousand feet, he rolled us upside down and before I could ask *why*, the intercom clicked.

"I'm looking for my cousin's ranch. It's easier to see what I'm looking for inverted. There it is, let's go say hi."

He reduced power to idle and killed the surplus altitude with graceful, swooping loops and rolls until we could see in the front room windows of a farmhouse as we zoomed by. Through my headset, I heard, "Rats! Wasted that buzz job, no one's home."

With the same negative result at the next cousin's ranch, Bob pulled up, added power that squished me into the seat and said, "Let's go back up and figure out where they've gone."

In the climb, I took an inventory of myself. "What do you know, calm, no butterflies. I musta grown up at last." Even the eight-year-old was quiet, and Dad's gold molar was invisible behind his satisfied expression.

Heat? Where's that heat coming from? From both sides of my seat, heat blew up from the small gap between the floor and the side walls. Of course, the radiator! My seat was over the radiator, and the lessons from "The Book," almost forgotten memories, returned in a flood. "Remember the story of the cooling system design?" I asked my fellow passengers, who smiled, pleased I hadn't forgotten.

Chug a, chug a, chug a, chug a, chug a... music by Rolls-Royce as the projector in my mind ran memories from books read in child-hood.

Move the cooling air inlet position down and out of the stagnant boundary layer next to the skin. To take advantage of the 'Meredith

Effect', the inlet ramp's divergent angle should be less than fifteen degrees to maintain dynamic pressure and still decelerate the airstream to maximize thermal transfer in the radiator core. An automatic, convergent exit duct, designed to restore airstream velocity and sustain perfect temperature, adds the radiator's waste heat energy to the airstream, squeezes the cooling air as it leaves the converging duct and gives the air one more push for a net gain in thrust. Seventy pounds of additional thrust is enough gain to neutralize the total drag of the cooling system.

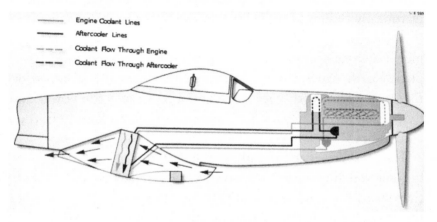

42. P-51 cooling system

From another book, I recalled,

The next big technology jump was to improve the radical, fussy, laminar flow airfoil. The P-51 was the first aircraft designed to use it; built with care, the increase in the total area of laminar flow in the boundary layer of air across the wing magically reduced drag. More speed.

Radical, blunt aileron trailing edges tamed the oscillating shockwave for improved roll control in a high-speed dive. The P-51 had perfectly balanced and harmonized controls, was the fastest fighter of World War II in level flight and, faster than any airplane of the time in a dive, could approach the speed of sound. All this, and the longest range of any fighter to see combat in WWII. The P-51 Mustang, with her long range, was a godsend for previously unescorted bomber crews being systematically slaughtered by defending enemy fighters.

Holy, moly! The books had been gone for half a century and the memories were still intact, the product of our combined recollection.

We've remembered everything.

This leap of technology from the drafting boards at North American delivered a second and often overlooked miraculous feature. By design, it was also relatively easy to fly. It had to be; there were no two-place P-51 trainers. Eighteen to twenty-year-old men, boys really, graduated from ponderous 450 horsepower, two-place North American AT-6 advanced trainers and strapped on this rocket ship with over three and a half times the power and twice the speed. They taught themselves to fly it, fight in it, then land it. Solo.

The consequence of failing the last course of training to become a fighter pilot in World War II, somewhat more severe than 'washing out,' was death. It's not for nothing we number these young men and a few mostly unsung women (WASPs, Women's Army Service Pilots) among "The Greatest Generation".

The design was neither evolutionary nor an improved model of an earlier version. Instead, an inspired and revolutionary airplane derived from a clean sheet of paper by North American Aircraft, a company that had never designed a fighter. Think about it, hundreds of people toiling night and day designed her without the aid of computers; pure slide rule and wind tunnel magic. The P-51 Mustang, a beloved icon of airplane people today, changed the world, saved the air war in Europe, and inspired generations of pilots and engineers. The real miracle is the incredibly short, one-hundred and two magical days from contract award to roll out.

Try that today.

Oh! My! God!

My head sagged from the induced "G" force of the pullout, 350 mph the last number I saw on the airspeed indicator as we dived for the runway at Sisters. We pulled out; Bob's cousin's barbecue and his aunt's hangar with her Twin Bonanza inside were both a blur when we flashed by in a banked, one wing low pass to give the crowd a look at this beautiful airplane.

43. Bob's P-51

With a flick of his wrist, he rolled level, tugged the stick, pushed the throttle, and the P-51 Mustang turned speed into altitude, lots of it, fast. The aroma of barbecue lingered in the cockpit.

The view out the windshield was all blue sky when I twisted in the seat, craning my head back to look down.

Man, it looks like the view from a rocket launch!

A clockwork of mottled brown and green earth rotated and retreated rapidly while we rolled and climbed straight up. Usually such a strain in the airplanes I fly, up was just another direction in this one.

We soared through ten thousand feet, pitched over backward and flew on inverted. The world in the top of the canopy, look up to see down had become normal, and I floated, happy in the heady intoxication of the shared passion from long ago. Layers of emotional corrosion induced by the bitter salts of disappointment, resentment, and self-pity flaked away.

The P-51 had done its work. Dad's gold molar gleamed in the sunlight, his infectious smile on high beam and my eight-year-old self was beside himself with the thrill of it all.

I'd waited a lifetime for this, yet there were no butterflies, no insane excitement, just an inner calm, cool as condensation on a glass of iced tea. Colonel Joe Cool was all grown up and a little disappointed to find it so.

We crossed the approach end of the runway at Redmond high and fast; midfield, banked hard left, a gut-wrenching, ninety-degree bank, a five hundred forty-degree overhead turn to burn off excess speed and altitude, and one last opportunity to spin the earth around a wingtip.

Some of the pre-landing checklist from the book sprang to mind when we rolled out on downwind. "Fuel on the fullest tank. Propeller, fine pitch. Mixture rich. Unlock the canopy. Gear down. Flaps down. Tailwheel locked." There must have been more, but before I could recall, the runway slid up to meet us, tires touched, mains first, chirp, chirp, followed closely by a third small chirp from the tailwheel.

Chug a, chug a, chug a, chug a, she still throbbed with the same pleasing sense of power as we taxied to the ramp. That's more than I could say for myself.

What is this?

Yikes, brain still functions, but my body's paralyzed. No, not paralyzed; I've been homogenized into a single-cell gelatinous mass; a sweating, heart pumping, breathing puddle of protoplasm.

Bob applied a little pressure to the right brake, and the airplane gracefully pirouetted around one wheel and came to a stop facing the runway. Brakes set, idle a minute to scavenge the oil. Mixture lean. Chug a, chug a, chu...silence. Switches off, click, click, click as the propeller blades coasted past the windshield and what remained of the adrenaline in my bloodstream drained away.

Bob rolled the canopy back, unbuckled his harness, hung the helmet on the canopy bow, stood up easily in the seat, nimbly climbed on the wing, and turned to see how I was doing. His grin faded to concern then returned when I grinned back like the Cheshire Cat. I looked around for my passengers, but Dad and that eight-year-old kid had gone off somewhere to enjoy a laugh at my expense.

"You gonna get out?"

"In a minute," I croaked.

Unsure how I got there, I stood on the wing where, before he helped me down, an alert crew member removed the headset and camera from my hands before they fell and damaged the precious plane.

"Are you okay? How was that?"

Speechless, I looked stupidly at him. "I'm fine; no, I'm great," I said as I lunged forward, wrapped him up, scooped him off his feet, and spun him around in the air while I sobbed. "I'm fine, I'm fine, thank you, thank you," I cried, then laughed hysterically.

My unflustered wife sat patiently with me at a picnic table and waited for me to return to sanity from uncontrolled tears and laughter, two sides of the same coin.

As I thought about it, I knew where those scoundrels, Dad and the eight-year-old, had gone. Nowhere!

The ride, after a lifetime apart, will let us live together permanently, rent-free in my mind.

44. *Jude, me, and Bob after my flight*

18.

"Damn Lucky Bugger!"

Enjoying the pleasure of my wife's fiftieth high school reunion, I watched the group from my self-assigned place by the food table and resisted the temptation to circulate. Rare and personal conversations blossomed when classmates figured out who was who then shared and compared life's surprises, good, bad or indifferent. Some of them who may not have had much in common as kids discovered common ground in sorrow, pain, or pleasure as aging adults.

I continued to wait and sampled the fruit plate while some, a little unsure of who I was, stole curious glances in my direction... "I don't know, he looks familiar..."

Some of them had seen me at previous reunions, but couldn't think of my name.

Curiosity eventually overcame reticence. Wrinkled brow, face screwed into a question, one of them approached me and asked, "I know I know you, but I can't think of your name. Did you move away before graduation?"

I'd had all evening to think about the question and prepared a simple answer to explain my presence with four words and a smile.

"I'm Judy Hodge's husband."

He nodded reflexively in unconscious agreement with the

thought that crossed his mind, a thought that betrayed him when it escaped through his slack-jawed open mouth in a low, quiet voice, "Ooooooh, Judy Hodge's husband."

I knew what he was thinking, could see it in his expression and heard it in his tone.

"Damn Lucky Bugger!"

My wife is one person they all immediately recognized. A petite and attractive young woman in high school, a cheerleader, a ballerina, band member, and friend with a sparkling intellect, she retained her kind heart, beauty, brains, figure, and electric smile. Best of all, she adopted my last name. He's right, I am...

"Damn Lucky Bugger."

45. Jude and me, early days in the Alon Aircoupe

PART III

THE BEGINNING

19.

Zig

September 1941, James Henley Dennis, fourteen years old, fades from the world of rational documents and will not re-emerge until February 1945. Even then, the records for the next several years of military service are incomprehensible.

Not that they don't exist, quite the contrary; instead of a quarter-inch sheaf of paper like most soldiers, his fragmented and partial history through all of World War II and beyond is two feet thick. According to Erik, a records research expert we contacted to decode them, none of it makes sense.

At first, a little naïve, I believed a search for my father's military experience would be a straightforward thing.

If I found Dad's reluctance to talk frustrating, I quickly learned others were equally displeased with my curiosity. A request for his service history met with stony silence until after many attempts, I was told, "They were lost in a fire in the St. Louis, Missouri storage facility in 1977."

The fire story was true enough, although by then, I'd found other ways to dig out information.

"If your father was ever injured while in the service, the Veterans Administration should have the medical records," suggested a friend.

They did, and at first the file appeared to be a treasure trove but, without additional information, proved more confusing than insightful.

Reinforcements

I need some help. Who, other than me, would be interested in stories about Germans frightened by my father?

Lightbulb!

Of course, the Nazi hunters from the Wiesenthal Center! The people there, very interested in the story of encounters with Germans, were disappointed Dad had been dead since 1977.

No use to the Center, they were nonetheless sympathetic to the bureaucratic roadblocks and promised, "The next time we go to Washington, D.C., we'll get your father's documents."

Now we're getting somewhere.

Weeks later, they called.

"We're very sorry. His records are unavailable, and we have a message for you."

"What's that?"

His answer, an echo of Dad's warning, *I'm afraid of Americans, and if we keep talking, you'd need to be, too.*

"Stop looking."

The Bowling Alley

Dad's stories of life on a cable-laying ship caused me to think.

The Coast Guard is the repository of all maritime documents; maybe they have some useful information.

Without a service number or the vessel's name, I wrote and requested records the Coast Guard assured me could not be found without this information.

Dang.

The only cables to cross an ocean that I knew of were laid in the Atlantic. While on the search for a transatlantic cable ship, something occurred to me that I'd not considered.

According to Dad's stories, he lived in Poulsbo and signed on with the ship early in the ninth grade.

How did a broke, abandoned kid get to the east coast?

Am I wrong? Might there have been a cable ship on the Pacific side of the country?

To answer the question, I turned to a resource even the comic book spaceman Buck Rogers lacked in 1941.

An internet search quickly revealed a single candidate, the privately owned and operated cable ship C.S. Restorer based out of Bamfield, B.C.

By 1939, the underwater cable from Seattle to military bases in Alaska had been allowed to degrade because the U.S. military planned to replace it with a less expensive radio system. In 1940, Japanese belligerence in Asia caused them to rethink this plan. In the event of a war with Japan, a radio system would not be as secure as a cable.

Plans were put in motion to repair and upgrade the cable. The Army Signal Corps leased the Restorer and assumed operation of the ship which sailed as a part of the Army Transport Service, the A.T.S. The crew was to be increased to one hundred thirty, housed in a new deckhouse.

There was one small hitch. Although many hundreds of competent seamen called the Seattle area home, all of them knew where the Restorer was headed, and few were interested in serving on a ship in winter on the notoriously dangerous Bering Sea. The additional crew would have to be recruited from a less well-informed source.

The old-world name for the process is "press-ganging," or "Shanghaiing." Lacing a man's drink with a drug, then bundling him onto a ship had gone out of style.

The modern equivalent: find men who had little or no choice other than to sign on for the voyage.

A local judge, regularly confronted with young men who'd come afoul of the law for minor infractions, agreed to do his patriotic duty and supply the warm bodies.

The history of the Restorer sounded like it might fit Dad's story.

Where was she docked in September 1941?

Her location on any given day should have been a simple matter of looking up the ship's logs, information habitually recorded by all maritime vessels, and permanently stored in the archives of the Coast Guard.

My request for the documents proved futile; the logs had mysteriously disappeared after the Signal Corps took control.

It was just another roadblock in my investigation until I read an obscure newspaper article which described the modifications made to the ship. As well as the new seamen's quarters, it mentioned the installation of a protective deck gun manned by an army crew.

An army crew, on a ship? Perhaps they kept records as well.

Another internet search uncovered what is described as 'rare gun logs' from the Restorer.

Whoever caused the ship's logs to disappear didn't know about the gun log.

This proved to be a home run. In September 1941, the C.S. Restorer was docked directly across the bay from Poulsbo, my father's home, and seat of the judge who hustled the young men into its service.

I think we've found Dad's cable ship.

Not so quick! What about the old answer to, "Where were you on December 7th, 1941?"

"Setting pins in a bowling alley" continued to be a problem.

Maybe it isn't a problem. It might be a clue.

In 1941, where were the bowling alleys on the west coast?

With the help of local historical societies, we found one bowling alley in, of all places, tiny Bamfield, British Columbia, and accessible only by boat or torturous automobile ride over ninety miles of primitive logging road.

How the heck did a bowling alley get there?

The answer, a bit of a surprise, was also a cautionary tale of assumption.

In 1902, the architect Francis Rattenbury who'd designed the B.C. Parliament Building and the Empress Hotel in Victoria had been commissioned to design a headquarters facility for the cable laying ship based at Bamfield.

Unlike urban Victoria located on the protected southeast tip of Vancouver Island, Bamfield is on the windswept west side, country mercilessly hammered by Pacific storms and little changed since first explored in 1792 by the Spanish explorer Dionisio Alcalá Galiano.

Rattenbury's design belonged in a modern city and included outdoor tennis courts where the weather might allow two days of play a year, a theater, and of course, a single lane, manual pin setting bowling alley.

The gun log provided the last nail in the coffin of our search for the ship.

Look at that, December 7th, 1941, the C.S. Restorer is moored to its home dock at the Bamfield Cable Station.

I needn't have mistrusted his story. Dad wasn't working in a bowling alley as I assumed but playing in one. He must have first heard of the attack while he took his turn resetting pins.

Self-congratulations for having proved he'd been on the Restorer were short lived. Within days, a thick manila envelope arrived in the mail with a return address from, of all organizations, the U.S. Navy.

After numerous requests, an anonymous someone sent a potpourri of records, most of which would turn out to be a pack of lies, but one unexpected document fell out and stole the wind from our sails. A handwritten letter to the Army from my straight-talking grandmother, and I paraphrase:

"Where the hell is my son? I used to send his mail to the C.S. Restorer, and now it comes back to me marked 'un-deliverable.'"

20.

Zag

ESP/eic

SPTAH 201 CPB.
10 June 1944

(Dennis, James H.) (Civ)
Mrs. Viola D. Olson
P.O. Box 595
Keyport, Washington

Dear Mrs. Olson:

This will acknowledge receipt of your letter of 2 June 1944 regarding your son, James Henly Dennis, an employee of this Port.

Any mail addressed to Mr. Dennis will reach him in care of Water Division, Seattle Port of Embarkation, 1519 South Alaskan Way, Seattle 4, Washington.

If this office can be of further service to you, please feel free to write.

Very truly yours,

HELEN E. BEAUCHAMP,
2nd Lt, TC (WAC),
Civilian Personnel Branch.

By 1944, my Grandma must have discovered that her 'take no hostages', hard-boiled Virginian temper, refined in the crucible of an orphanage, didn't play well with government servants. What she actually wrote follows.

Keyport, Wn,
June 2, 1944

S.P.O.E.
Officer in charge –
Dear Sir,
I am writing you in regards to my son, James Henley Dennis. His address until recently was U.S.S. Restorer – c/o Fleet Postmaster, San Francisco, Calif. He was recently transferred to Prince Rupert or I think that was where he was sent, that was nearly three weeks ago and I haven't heard from him, and don't know where to write him. Can you please give me his address. Thank you,

His mother
Viola Dennis Olson
PO Box #595
Keyport, Wn.

Wow! Dad, a master of double speak, couldn't hold a candle to Helen Beauchamp who'd adroitly answered Viola's question without telling her a thing. Ironically, if my calculations are even close, Grandma has called her son's disappearance with surprising accuracy.

Weeks before she penned her letter, his twisted records imply he shipped out to an unknown destination, but not before he sent her a coded message in a poem that got past the censors. His dear old ma put it in the local paper as she often did with family comings and goings.

Dear Mother,
> *Just a note to let you know*
> *That things are still O.K.*
> *And letters soon will follow,*
> *Maybe one for every day.*
>
> *Right now I'm blue and lonely,*
> *With nothing much to write,*
> *For we're restricted to the camp*
> *And cannot see a sight.*
>
> *Our time we hardly call our own,*
> *There's little else but work,*
> *And though it makes not much for news,*
> *It's something we cannot shirk.*
>
> *So even though my letters lag*
> *And this is but a poem,*
> *I carry but a single thought-*
> *That soon I will be home*
> *To say, I love you.*
> *JAMES*

'Restricted to the camp', 'cannot see a sight', and 'little else but work'? Work? Work at what, and why restricted to the camp? As far as that goes, what's an underage kid who's supposed to be on a ship in the Bering Sea doing in a camp?

In 1944, Viola was still sending letters to her Jimmy on the C.S. Restorer – c/o Fleet Postmaster, San Francisco, Calif., although the Restorer was, as Helen corrected, based out of Seattle.

Jimmy signed onto the Restorer in September 1941 and sent letters to his mother in Virginia until she moved back to Keyport, WA and remarried. By June 1944, she thinks he's still on the Restorer and sending her letters in care of the ship even though he received an Honorable Discharge from the Army Transportation Service in January 1942.

What Helen meant was, "Sorry Viola, Jimmy is at sea, out of town, away, incommunicado, no more awkward letters full of doublespeak; he'll contact you when he returns, stop asking."

By now I'm not the least surprised to uncover, ah, snags in the fragmented records collected from unexpected sources. The Coast Guard can't produce maritime documents for service on an A.T.S. ship, but the Army does. The Air Force can't find his file but has some medical records, and the local police department can read over the phone the details of an accident record from 1948 but can't send a transcript because "We don't keep records from that far back."

Best of all, out of the blue, the Army coughed up what Dad could never get for himself, credit for service in WWII, an honorable discharge from the Army Transport Service for his service in 1944.

Although I'd never asked the Army for a discharge, they apparently unearthed the same documents I'd found that described James' role on two ships.

First, his undefined role on one of two Rosebanks, either a vessel out of Vancouver leased by the A.T.S. or one requisitioned from the Dutch under duress, which sailed under a swastika for the balance of the war. Then the F-49, for which no record exists.

Another document says the F-49 sailed to the Southwest Pacific where James earned double pay for hazardous duty.

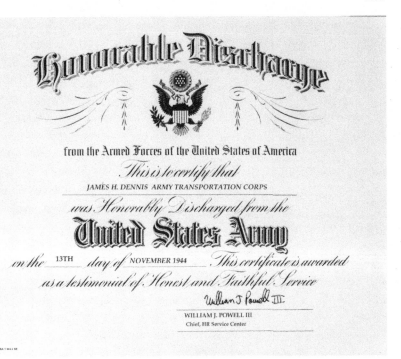

Honorable Discharge

from the Armed Forces of the United States of America

This is to certify that

JAMES H. DENNIS ARMY TRANSPORTATION CORPS

was Honorably Discharged from the

United States Army

on the ___13TH___ day of ___NOVEMBER 1944___ This certificate is awarded as a testimonial of Honest and Faithful Service

William J Powell III

WILLIAM J. POWELL III
Chief, HR Service Center

46. *Finally, an acknowledgment for service in WWII, this is at least his second Honorable Discharge from the ATS, Nov 13, 1944.*

21.

Zig, Again

Dear Sirs, Thank you so much for the honorable discharge for my father's service in WWII. Our family is pleased and proud of the recognition, and now, respectfully request a Victory medal and ribbon, which they eventually sent.

There's nothing quite so stimulating as success, no matter how fraudulent. I decided to push a little more.

Dear Sirs,

Thank you for recognizing my father's service and for the Victory medal. Would you be so kind as to supply us with a record of where he sailed on these ships so it can be determined which theater medal he qualifies for, the SW Pacific, or the European/North African?

Thundering silence followed.

The conundrum is complicated by a previous honorable discharge from the ATS in January 1942.

Before this is over, his time in the ATS will become even more confused.

Officialdom no help, or worse; it's back to basics. Return to the beginning and sort this out, piece by piece.

Not an historical document, the honorable discharge is new in 2016. It arrived with the three letters that follow.

CAUTION: NOT TO BE USED FOR IDENTIFICATION PURPOSES
THIS IS AN IMPORTANT RECORD. SAFEGUARD IT.
ANY ALTERATIONS IN SHADED AREAS RENDER FORM VOID

CERTIFICATE OF RELEASE OR DISCHARGE FROM ACTIVE DUTY
This Report Contains Information Subject to the Privacy Act of 1974, As Amended.

1. NAME (Last, First, Middle) DENNIS, JAMES H	2. DEPARTMENT, COMPONENT AND BRANCH ARMY/ATC	3. SOCIAL SECURITY NUMBER

4a. GRADE, RATE OR RANK N/A	b. PAY GRADE N/A	5. DATE OF BIRTH (YYYYMMDD) 19261206	6. RESERVE OBLIGATION TERMINATION DATE (YYYYMMDD) 00000000

7a. PLACE OF ENTRY INTO ACTIVE DUTY N/A	b. HOME OF RECORD AT TIME OF ENTRY (City and state, or complete address if known) N/A

8a. LAST DUTY ASSIGNMENT AND MAJOR COMMAND ARMY TRANSPORTATION CORPS	b. STATION WHERE SEPARATED FORT KNOX, KY

9. COMMAND TO WHICH TRANSFERRED N/A	10. SGLI COVERAGE X NONE AMOUNT: $

11. PRIMARY SPECIALTY (List number, title and years and months in specialty. List additional specialty numbers and titles involving periods of one or more years.) NONE//NOTHING FOLLOWS	12. RECORD OF SERVICE	YEAR(S)	MONTH(S)	DAY(S)
	a. DATE ENTERED AD THIS PERIOD	1944	05	12
	b. SEPARATION DATE THIS PERIOD	1944	11	13
	c. NET ACTIVE SERVICE THIS PERIOD	0000	06	02
	d. TOTAL PRIOR ACTIVE SERVICE	0000	00	00
	e. TOTAL PRIOR INACTIVE SERVICE	0000	00	00
	f. FOREIGN SERVICE	0000	06	02
	g. SEA SERVICE	0000	00	00
	h. INITIAL ENTRY TRAINING	0000	00	00
	i. EFFECTIVE DATE OF PAY GRADE	0000	00	00

13. DECORATIONS, MEDALS, BADGES, CITATIONS AND CAMPAIGN RIBBONS AWARDED OR AUTHORIZED (All periods of service) NONE//NOTHING FOLLOWS	14. MILITARY EDUCATION (Course title, number of weeks, and month and year completed) NONE//NOTHING FOLLOWS

15a. COMMISSIONED THROUGH SERVICE ACADEMY	YES	X NO
b. COMMISSIONED THROUGH ROTC SCHOLARSHIP (10 USC Sec. 2107b)	YES	X NO
c. ENLISTED UNDER LOAN REPAYMENT PROGRAM (10 USC Chap. 109) (If Yes, years of commitment NA)	YES	X NO

16. DAYS ACCRUED LEAVE PAID 0	17. MEMBER WAS PROVIDED COMPLETE DENTAL EXAMINATION AND ALL APPROPRIATE DENTAL SERVICES AND TREATMENT WITHIN 90 DAYS PRIOR TO SEPARATION	YES	NO X

18. REMARKS
PERIODS OF ACTIVE DUTY: 19440512-19440903 USAT ROSEBANK//19440904-19441113 P 49//THIS DOCUMENT ISSUED UNDER PL 95-202 (38 USC 106 NOTE) ADMINISTRATIVELY ESTABLISHES ACTIVE DUTY SERVICE FOR THE PURPOSES OF DEPARTMENT AFFAIRS BENEFITS//DD FORM 214 ADMINISTRATIVELY ISSUED ON 20160202//NOTHING FOLLOWS

The information contained herein is subject to computer matching within the Department of Defense or with any other affected Federal or non-Federal agency for verification purposes and to determine eligibility for, and/or continued compliance with, the requirements of a Federal benefit program.

19a. MAILING ADDRESS AFTER SEPARATION (Include ZIP Code) N/A	b. NEAREST RELATIVE (Name and address - include ZIP Code) MICHAEL R DENNIS

20. MEMBER REQUESTS COPY 6 BE SENT TO (Specify state/locality) NA	OFFICE OF VETERANS AFFAIRS X YES NO
a. MEMBER REQUESTS COPY 3 BE SENT TO THE CENTRAL OFFICE OF THE DEPARTMENT OF VETERANS AFFAIRS (WASHINGTON, DC)	YES X NO

21.a. MEMBER SIGNATURE NOT AVAILABLE TO SIGN	b. DATE (YYYYMMDD)	22.a. OFFICIAL AUTHORIZED TO SIGN (Typed name, grade, title, signature) SIGNED BY: ROBERTS.NAOMI.JARUSHA.1181333274 NAOMI J ROBERTS, GS07, HUMAN RESOURCE ASSIST	b. DATE (YYYYMMDD) 20160202

SPECIAL ADDITIONAL INFORMATION (For use by authorized agencies only)

23. TYPE OF SEPARATION DISCHARGE	24. CHARACTER OF SERVICE (Include upgrades) HONORABLE

25. SEPARATION AUTHORITY PL 95-202	26. SEPARATION CODE N/A	27. REENTRY CODE N/A

28. NARRATIVE REASON FOR SEPARATION N/A

29. DATES OF TIME LOST DURING THIS PERIOD (YYYYMMDD) NONE	30. MEMBER REQUESTS COPY 4 (Initials)

DD FORM 214, AUG 2009	PREVIOUS EDITION IS OBSOLETE. GENERATED BY ARBA	MEMBER - 4

47. Honorable Discharge record from the Army Transportation Corps, Feb 2, 2016.

DEPARTMENT OF THE ARMY
U.S. ARMY HUMAN RESOURCES COMMAND
1600 SPEARHEAD DIVISION AVENUE, DEPARTMENT 480
FORT KNOX, KY 40122-5408

APR 1 3 2016

Awards and Decorations Branch

Mr. Michael R. Dennis

Dear Mr. Dennis:

This is in response to your letter concerning your desire to obtain any award that your late father, Mr. James H. Dennis may be entitled to for his service in World War II as well as historical information about his service on board the USAT Rosebank.

Based upon a review of the documentation submitted and available to this office, we were able to verify his entitlement to the World War II Victory Medal as well as the Honorable Service Lapel Button.

We are also unable to issue a DD Form 215 (Correction to Report of Separation) as the DD Form 214 (Report of Separation) issued for your father has missing information needed to generate the DD Form 215. We have, however, forwarded a Memorandum for Record reflecting his entitlement to these awards to the National Personnel Records Center for inclusion in his Army Military Human resource Record. This Memorandum is an official document and may be used for the same purposes as a DD Form 215.

The regulatory policy governing the Awards and Decorations Branch is very explicit with regards to eligibility for issuance of awards and decorations. Awards may only be issued to the Veteran or to the Veteran's primary next of kin in the following order: un-remarried spouse, eldest surviving child, father or mother, eldest surviving sibling, and eldest surviving grandchild.

In this regard, we were unable to determine whether you are Mr. Dennis's primary next of kin. In order to receive these medals, we require documentation reflecting your status as the primary next of kin, as described above. If you are not the primary next of kin, you may provide us with a privacy release signed by the primary next of kin, authorizing you to receive these medals on their behalf. We have enclosed a sample privacy release form.

48. Acknowledgment of service aboard the Rosebank.

-2-

Additionally, if you wish to learn more about your father's service on board the USAT Rosebank, you will need to contact the United States Army Center of Military History. You may write their office at: U.S. Army Center of Military History, 102 4th Avenue, Building 35, Fort McNair, District of Columbia, 20319-5060. You may also email them at: usarmy.mcnair.cmh.mbx.answers@mail.mil.

It is an honor to verify these awards in recognition of your father's faithful and dedicated service to our Nation during a time of great need.

Sincerely,

Wil B. Neubauer
Lieutenant Colonel, U.S. Army
Chief, Awards and Decorations Branch

Enclosures

49. Page 2

50. WWII Victory Medal & Honorable Service lapel pin

DEPARTMENT OF THE ARMY
U.S. ARMY HUMAN RESOURCES COMMAND
1600 SPEARHEAD DIVISION AVENUE, DEPARTMENT 420
FORT KNOX, KY 40122-5402

February 2, 2016

Human Resource Service Center

Mr. Michael R. Dennis

Dear Mr. Dennis:

I am pleased to inform you that your application for Mr. James H. Dennis discharge under the provisions of Public Law 95-202 and/or Public Law 105-368 has been approved for his participation in the Army Transportation Corps.

Enclosed are the Certificate of Honorable Discharge DD Form 256A, and Certificate of Release or Discharge from Active Duty DD Form 214.

If there are any corrections concerning the enclosed documents please forward them to the above address. Any benefits to which you may be entitled based upon Mr. Dennis' service would be administered by the Department of Veterans Affairs. It is suggested that you contact the nearest office of that agency for information concerning such benefits.

Mr. Dennis' service to our country in time of war is deeply appreciated. Enclosed you will find a letter from the Chief of Transportation acknowledging his dedicated service. If you require additional information, please contact us.army.knox.hrc.mbx.tagd-ask-hrc@mail.mil, call (888) 276-9472 or write to: U.S. Army Human Resources Command Attention: Human Resource Service Center, 1600 Spearhead Division Avenue, Department 420, Fort Knox, KY 40122-5402.

Sincerely,

Shun P. Thomas
Supervisor, Veterans Inquiry Supervisor
Human Resource Service Center

Enclosures

51. Benefits I'd be entitled to because of my father's service? Someone thought my quest for information was a fishing expedition for money.

DEPARTMENT OF THE ARMY
OFFICE OF THE CHIEF OF TRANSPORTATION
2221 ADAMS AVENUE
FORT LEE, VIRGINIA 23801-2102

REPLY TO
ATTENTION OF

FEB 2 - 2016

Chief of Transportation

Dear Veteran:

On behalf of Army Transporters throughout history and their many decades of dedication to the defense of our nation, I take this opportunity to thank you for your service in the World War II seagoing Army Transport Service. Your service has now been duly recognized as having veteran's status, an outstanding tribute to your accomplishments aboard United States Army transports in ocean service or in foreign waters during World War II.

You are a vital part of the Army's marine transportation heritage and traditions. You may be aware that we had more floating units in World War II than did the United States Navy, and it was in operation prior to the creation of the Continental Navy. Today, as in your day, the US Army Transportation Corps Regiment encompasses a superb collection of young men and women in the mariner field. They are carrying on the outstanding heritage you developed during your service. You can be proud of their successes as we have been of yours.

We are continually renewing our commitment to the Army's mission in the defense of our nation. We have recently modernized our fleet of watercraft, and our ocean-going vessels now have the capability to meet logistics-over-the shore operations in any geographic location where necessary. These improvements were born out of experiences of members of the Army Transport Service like yourself.

Your service and dedication are very much appreciated, and your recognized status as a World War II veteran justifiably deserved. The personnel of the Transportation Corps salute you and wish you nothing but the best.

Sincerely,

Stephen E. Farmen
Brigadier General, US Army
Chief of Transportation

SAIL ARMY
SPEARHEAD

52. Oh goodness, look at that, did anyone tell General Farman, James is dead?

22.

Through the Looking
Glass

By way of his own story and the letter from his mother, Jimmy
Dennis became James H. Dennis when drawn into the clutches of
government service aboard the cable ship Restorer sometime after
the middle of September 1941.

He was setting pins in the bowling alley at the Restorer's headquarters in Bamfield, BC on December 7, 1941.

Exactly when did he sign on?

A history of the Signal Corps gives up a clue.

A unique and fortunate decision taken in connection with the
Northwest defense needs was to recondition and restore to use the
Alaskan cable. The cable ship Restorer sailed from Victoria on
October 7th, repaired breaks at Resurrection Bay and the Seward
cable landing, sailed into a gale at Ketchikan, the terminal point
for the Seward cable to the northwest and the Seattle cable to the
southeast, yet managed to complete the work by the first week of
November. Just before Pearl Harbor, cable took its place as the cen-
tral link between General DeWitt's Fourth Army headquarters at the
Presidio of San Francisco. A telephone land line was used between
Anchorage and Seward, then the cable to Seattle, and then a teletype

circuit to San Francisco. The cable restoration was fortunate not only that it provided a secure transmission means when the surprise at Pearl Harbor shook security, but also because it provided almost the only one. For despite promises, the administrative radio network was not ready until mid-1942. *(http://tothosewhoserved.org/usa/ts/ usatss01/chapter11.html).*

There it was, as close as we'll get. Sometime between September 3rd and October 7th, as we suspected, Jimmy became a crew member of the Restorer, service for which a special law had been enacted to allow men between sixteen and seventeen-and-a-half, boys really, to serve on ships of the A.T.S.

Jimmy was fourteen.

The Hookah Smok'n Caterpillar

The ninth grader who served on the C.S. Restorer without distinction from September 1941 until discharged from the A.T.S. three months later, January 3rd, 1942, had celebrated his fifteenth birthday the day before the attack on Pearl Harbor.

I assumed the short service time implied discovery of his underage condition; an Honorable Discharge said otherwise. In the document, over the line labeled 'Previous Service', is typed TWO YEARS.

The Honorable Discharge is only the first of hundreds of confusing documents that comprise a record of misdirection that would ripple far into the future.

Second Son of a Ghost

By Jim Dennis
(My *brother*)

My history of espionage.

In the fall of 1972, I made a decision which would affect far more than just addressing the question every teenager asks, "What will I do with my future?"

As I began my senior year of high school, the Vietnam War was ending in a very confused state. While it looked like the draft would end within the next 12 months, it might not happen before my graduation. Without the grades necessary for college and no desire to continue school, I made plans to join the military with as much control as a 17-year-old might have. The Army, Marines, and Navy had no appeal at all, which left the Air Force as the only option. A quick-talking recruiter assured me that while he had no openings for air traffic controllers then, by enlisting early I could cross-train as soon as an opening presented itself.

I remember the recruiter filling out the paperwork over our kitchen table with Dad in attendance. At some point in the conversation, the recruiter briefly mentioned that the career field I had chosen would require a deep background investigation for the required security clearance. As we finished the paperwork and bid goodbye, Dad's parting comment was, "Well this ought to be interesting." It would be five years before I'd better understand his concerns.

Six months later, in the summer of 1973, I joined the Air Force and after an abbreviated Basic Training (four days instead of six weeks, which is a whole other story) I found myself in temporary quarters waiting for my technical school to begin. My security clearance was delayed for unknown issues but finally approved in August, and I headed for Keesler Air Force Base in Biloxi, Mississippi.

After training, during the first five years of enlistment my duty stations were at the National Security Agency, Fort Devens, Massachusetts, Wright Patterson Air Force Base, the Air Force Academy, and Clear Air Force Station in Alaska.

In the spring of 1979 near the end of my six-year tour, my last duty station was the Strategic Air Command in Omaha, Nebraska. I had been interviewing with a variety of companies that wanted to avail themselves of the security clearances I had been issued.

I returned to my barracks room one evening where I found a business card bearing the seal of the D.I.A., "Defense Intelligence Agency," pinned to my door. The card bore a note with an office location where I "had" an appointment. The agent I met with the next day wanted to discuss "off the record" some issues they had found during the renewal of my security clearances.

My dad had died two years earlier, and the agent began by informing me that my initial clearance had been delayed five years earlier by issues the D.I.A. had with dad's military records. His records were unavailable to them because they had been sealed, along with the Nuremberg War Crimes Trial records, by presidential seal following WWII. When I asked him why they were sealed, he could give no reason other than the D.I.A. was assured that there was nothing in his records that would prevent his son from having a Top Secret Clearance.

He did recommend that I continue to ask for copies of his records when they were next scheduled to be released in 25 years. He also mentioned that in his 20 years as a D.I.A. agent, he'd never had records refused for their review!

Six years later when I left Lockheed Corporation to marry and move to the Midwest, I signed a non-travel agreement with the government which placed a 12-year hold on my passport that prevented my traveling outside the United States. I remember years later talking with friends who had left corporate service and found that they had not had the same restriction placed on them as I had, even though we basically performed the same work and had access to the same classified information.

Maybe it wasn't what I knew but what Dad knew?

Jim Dennis

Jim Dennis Jr., son of the Rev. and Mrs. James H. Dennis. 828 N. 9th Ave.. recently enlisted in the U.S. Air Force. according to M. Sgt. Don Lish. local Air Force recruiter.

Dennis enlisted for a guaranteed job as an electronic emissions monitor analysis specialist and is now taking six weeks basic training with the Air Force School of Military Science at Lackland AFB. San Antonio. Tex.

Recruiter Lish is at the Walla Walla Area Chamber of Commerce building each Wednesday from 1 to 4 p.m.

Jim Dennis

53. June 15, 1973 Walla Walla Union-Bulletin

23.

A Hole in Time

Meanwhile, back in 1941, December 8, the United States declared war on Japan, and the Restorer is ordered to Seattle where the crew is conscripted into the Army Transport Service. Three days later, on the 11th, the country is engulfed in another World War when Germany and Italy declare war on the United States.

From Seattle, the logs are fuzzy; the Restorer sailed to an unknown destination and returned prior to January 9th. We know she returned before the 9th because James was granted an honorable discharge from the A.T.S. on January 3, 1942.

Although I've accumulated hundreds of pages of related documents, I have been no more successful at acquiring his records than the D.I.A.

A hole in time, eleven months and eight days, exists between his exit from A.T.S. service and his reappearance on December 11, 1942, the same year the first mass-produced, detailed model airplane kits were delivered to hobby shops.

In light of what I understand of Dad's wartime activity, his stories have proven reliable, so I assumed the hole was filled with related activity.

He needed a job, the country was at war, and he was doing essential work maintaining the cable. Why would he leave the ship unless someone recruited him for something more interesting?

I wonder who?

A simple application for a job dated 10/14/42 offered up a clue. Under 'Personal References,' James lists three; two unremarkable, and one very unlikely.

Reference: Harry J. Hansen
Business: Commander U.S. Navy
Length of Acquaintance: 2 years

Two years? How does a thirteen-year-old know an officer in the U.S. Navy; who, exactly, is Commander Hansen, and what is their relationship?

With a new name to search, it didn't take long to shed light on the question. Commander Hansen had been assigned to the Restorer. The Restorer was operated by The Signal Corps who functioned under the direction of and developed electronic gadgets for the O.S.S., Office of Strategic Services, predecessor of the C.I.A.

To protect their agents' identities, the O.S.S. used the A.T.S. and its convoluted record system to obfuscate records of personnel involved in the clandestine service.

In WWII, the movement of ships at sea is a closely held secret. "Jimmy is at sea; he'll let you know when he returns."

As Helen Beauchamp implied, don't ask.

"Loose lips sink ships."

From January 1939 to June 21, 1940, James' father worked for the Signal Corps, and this may explain how a kid knew a Navy commander. If he really did know the Commander for two years, then they met a year before James signed on the Restorer, precisely the time period Clarence also worked for the Signal Corps.

Our country lacked an intelligence service; the Japanese attack at Pearl Harbor on December 7, 1941, highlighted the need, so the government organized a group to build one. The O.S.S. officially came into being in September 1942, but Mr. Donovan, Roosevelt's Coordinator of Information and future director of the O.S.S. had already been scouring the services for employees and agents for many months.

Might Commander Hansen, the man in command of the Restorer's crew, representative of the Signal Corps, be a recruiter on a search for talent to fill the ranks and help fulfill the schemes of the O.S.S.?

Declassified, the O.S.S. membership roster is available today; a James H. Dennis is on the list.

I'm speculating here, but in a time of crisis, who would one reach out to first, and trust most, but someone you already know?

To discover more about Mr. Hansen, I returned to the impossible-to-foresee internet for the answer.

Commander Hansen served for forty-two years and rose to the rank of Rear Admiral.

Oh, just how cool is that? This guy is gonna have a record as thick as your arm.

A Google search for details of any senior officer, no matter how obscure, produces pages of his history; however, a search for information about Rear Admiral Harry J. Hansen unearthed one single reference.

Birth: March 24th, 1888
Death: March 6, 1984
RADM
U.S. NAVY
WORLD WAR I & II

The page also included a picture of his gravestone.

To date, only requests for my father's service record had produced less information.

Harry was a friend of the family and probably the recruiter who plucked Dad from the Restorer.

Deductive Reasoning

On the search, we occasionally found records of people doing similar work; clear, concise, efficient, they speak only of the facts, and never offer conjecture or opinion. Although there are significant and conflicting records for 1943, 44, 45, 46, and 1947, most of 1942 is strangely devoid of documents after fifteen-year-old James is granted an Honorable discharge from the A.T.S. with two years of service credit for three months on the C.S. Restorer.

Why the blank time?

As we unearthed records, it appeared that he'd been abandoned by his mother who fled to family in Virginia when her husband died. This is unlikely; she and James had a close relationship. She would not have left until he had an income and a place to live. I can't be certain because I don't have the exact date of either his enlistment in the service of the Restorer or Grandma's departure date, but they appear to coincide. I'm sure before her departure, Viola was satisfied the needs of her young teenager would be met by employment on the Restorer. Jimmy was both working for and living on the ship.

Even though Viola's return to Keyport corresponds with James' exit from the A.T.S., until long after the war he never again lived with her, which begs the question, 'Where was his home in 1942?' Since there are no records of this time, the answer must surely lie in the story he told me.

"I was placed in the home of a German-speaking family in the Midwest and wasn't allowed to eat until I could ask for the potatoes in perfect German."

The question I never asked then is important now, "Whose home?"

Work backward. The decision whether to participate or not was rudely taken away from a country unprepared for war. Time was of the essence; who did the persons tasked with building an intelligence apparatus personally know and trust? Who was available that could be enlisted to help right now and had the skills to train James in German so perfect he couldn't be tripped up by using the wrong dialect?

I may be wrong, but all my research screams, "Don't look too far, they were practical people who lived in small towns and knew each other intimately."

A likely candidate springs from the pages of the records. A witness on the marriage certificate for both Viola and her new husband, Oscar, is Carl A. Darsow. Carl's parents emigrated from Germany and were living in Minnesota. Who better to teach the German dialects than recently arrived Germans, parents of a friend?

I think James was off to Minnesota for rapid, full-immersion language training. Learn quickly or starve. Even if I'm wrong about Carl's family participation, someone provided it because, with zero background in foreign language, my father ended up with a brilliant command of all aspects of the German language.

As noted before, there was no effort to adulterate his records during this time. Nothing confusing or odd, there are just no records, quite unlike the years following which are so full of mischief, they sound like a farce.

The work history that follows can only be regarded as entertainment, or James was the worst employee ever hired by the U.S. Government to work in a torpedo station, or two shipyards a thousand miles apart. Maybe someone wanted him to look like a dufus so no other government employer would try to hire him away.

Your guess is as good as mine.

Affidavit of Male Applicant for Marriage License

STATE OF WASHINGTON,
County of Kitsap, } ss.

MUST BE FILLED IN BY MALE APPLICANT

The undersigned, being first duly sworn, deposes as follows: That I am the **MALE** applicant for the issuance of a marriage license by the County Auditor of Kitsap County, State of Washington. I am not feeble-minded, an imbecile, insane, epileptic, a common drunkard, we are not related and I am not afflicted with pulmonary tuberculosis in its advanced stages nor with contagious venereal disease and that I am..54...years of age. Color..white..

Occupation..Classified Labor.......... Birthplace..Iowa, Manly,..

Single..Yes.... Widowed..no.... Divorced..no.... Name of Guardian..............

Signature..Oscar Olson.......... Address..Box 512 Keyport..

..Washington..

Subscribed and sworn to before me this......6.......day of......Nov......, 19.42

..Nell Schoch..

Deputy Auditor, Kitsap County, Washington.

or Notary Public residing at..............

Affidavit of Female Applicant for Marriage License

STATE OF WASHINGTON,
County of Kitsap, } ss.

MUST BE FILLED IN BY FEMALE APPLICANT

The undersigned, being first duly sworn, deposes as follows: That I am the **FEMALE** applicant for the issuance of a marriage license by the County Auditor of Kitsap County, State of Washington. I am not feeble-minded, an imbecile, insane, epileptic, a common drunkard, we are not related and I am not afflicted with pulmonary tuberculosis in its advanced stages and that I am..44......years of age.

Color..white...... Occupation..housewife. Birthplace..Virginia..

Single..yes.... Widowed..yes.... Divorced..no.... Name of Guardian..............

Signature..Viola Ethel Dennis.......... Address..Rt 595 Keyport..

..Washington..

Subscribed and sworn to before me this......6.......day of......Nov......, 19.42

..Nell Schoch..

Deputy Auditor, Kitsap County, Washington.

or Notary Public residing at..............

STATE OF WASHINGTON,
County of Kitsap, } ss.

Affidavit of Witness

The undersigned, being first duly sworn, deposes and says: That I am personally acquainted with

..Oscar Olson.......... of ..Keyport.. Wash
Name of Male Applicant / Bonafide Residence

who is..54...years of age; and with

..Viola Ethel Dennis.......... of ..Keyport.. Wash
Name of Female Applicant / Bonafide Residence

who is..44......years of age; that neither of said persons is a habitual criminal or related and I know of no legal impediment to their being joined in marriage.

Witness for Both Parties:

Name..Carl A. Darsow.......... Address..Rt #1 Box 1315 Bremerton, Wash

Subscribed and sworn to before me this......6.......day of......Nov......, 19.42

..Nell Schoch..

Deputy Auditor, Kitsap County, Washington.

or Notary Public residing at..............

Date of Application..Nov 6, 1942.......Date License Issued..Nov 10, 1942..License No...14933

Mailed Mon A M 11-9-42

Mail to female applicant at above address

450

54. Carl Darsow was a witness when Grandma Ethel remarried

PART IV

THE RECORDS

24.

Dec 1942–Feb 1945

Friday, Dec 11, 1942.

JAMES HENLEY DENNIS HIRED AS A MECHANIC
LEARNER, $4.64 PER DAY. NAVAL TORPEDO STATION,
KEYPORT, WA.

An application for work states he's lived at PO Box 595, Keyport WA, for two years and has never been employed. Listed as a reference on his application is Harry J. Hansen, Commander, U.S. Navy who he claims to have known for two years. James states on later records that he had worked as a porter at Black Ball Ferry Station in Seattle, WA in 1941.

Oh yeah, forgot about that job... and his time on the Restorer.

Monday, Dec 14, 1942.

Began work at Keyport Naval Torpedo Station.
Third shift.

Employees worked Monday through Saturday with Sundays off.
It wasn't long before he let his employer know what he was made of.

55. *Keyport Torpedo Station*

Wednesday, Dec 23, 1942.

INJURY. REASON: PULLING LEVER DOWN ON DRILL
PRESS AND SPRAINED WRIST. PAIN IN WRIST, SLIGHT
SWELLING. RECOMMEND RETURN TO WORK.

*Sprained his wrist pulling the handle of a drill press? What a fanciful
idea. I've been a machinist for forty-five years. There are many ways to
sprain a wrist; pulling the handle of a drill press isn't one of them.*

Thursday, Dec 31, 1942.

EMPLOYEE IS NOT CAPABLE OF MORE ADVANCED WORK.

This guy is just too damn dumb. More advanced than what?

Sunday, Jan 3, 1943.

ABSENT FROM WORK WITHOUT PERMISSION. ON SICK
LEAVE WITH FLEU. CHECKED OUT THROUGH OFFICE.
STATEMENT UNTRUE, NO ONE TO VALIDATE. ABSENCE

APPROVED.

I don't get it.

Sunday, Feb 7, 1943.

SICK LEAVE. REASON: FLEU.

Again. The employee of record supposedly filled out the form himself. James has excellent spelling skills and does not misspell simple words like 'flu'.

Sunday, Feb 28, 1943.

EMPLOYEE IS NOT CAPABLE OF MORE ADVANCED WORK.

In case you didn't get the memo from December 31st.

March 1943.

Incongruously, the Kitsap Herald announced that he left for service in Germany. As far as we can tell, he's not in any service; sixteen, and too young to sign up. His mother, Viola Ethel has a history of letting the local paper know of all significant, or insignificant events at her house. Why she might have thought Jimmy left the country is a mystery.

Monday, May 3, 1943.

ABSENT FROM WORK WITHOUT PERMISSION FOR TWO HOURS. REASON: THE ALARM CLOCK JUST WASN'T LOUD ENOUGH. SUSPENDED FOR ONE DAY, THURSDAY, MAY 7TH. ANSWER CONSIDERED UNSATISFACTORY.

Not just incompetent, but, ah, imaginative.

Tuesday, May 25, 1943.

ABSENT. REASON: I HAVE OIL POISONING AND MY
HANDS WERE ITCHING. LEAVE NOT APPROVED. 'OIL
POISONING' IS NOT GROUNDS FOR ABSENTEEISM.

Sensitive skin.

Saturday, May 29, 1943.

REPORTED TO WORK WITHOUT BADGE. CONSIDERED
ABSENT. REASON: I CHANGED SHIRTS AND FORGOT TO
TAKE MY BADGE OFF THE DIRTY SHIRT.

Slow, incompetent, lazy, and forgetful, too.

Sunday, May 30, 1943.

ABSENT FROM WORK WITHOUT PERMISSION. FORGOT
BADGE AGAIN.

*This just gets better and better. Moe's on the job, now all we need is Curly,
and Larry.*

Monday, May 31, 1943.

ABSENT FROM WORK WITHOUT PERMISSION. HAD TO
TAKE MOTHER TO BREMERTON.

But a good son.

Tuesday, June 1, 1943.

ABSENT FROM WORK WITHOUT PERMISSION. TOOK
MOTHER TO DOCTOR.

*Again? Either Mother is a hypochondriac, or Jimmy likes to go for a
drive.*

Tuesday, June 8, 1943.

REQUESTED RESIGNATION "TO GO TUNA FISHING."
RELEASE NOT RECOMMENDED. NOT APPROVED FOR
EMPLOYMENT ELSEWHERE.

James left anyway.
Who wouldn't rather go fishing?

Friday, June 18, 1943.

SEPARATION GRANTED.

Of course it was, he earned it.

NOTE: O.S.S. training took six months. December 1942 until
he left for California in June 1943 = six months. Coincidence?

Monday, June 28, 1943.

EMPLOYED AS A HELPER AT U.S. NAVAL DRYDOCKS,
TERMINAL ISLAND, CA.

He lived with his older brother Bill and his wife Jane, or at least
used their address. Bill's handwriting was on James' application
for employment.

There's a backstory to his time at Terminal Island. It didn't happen, and I know this not from the records that are all written
in his brother's handwriting, or that the basic information is all
wrong, but from a personal encounter with Aunt Jane in 1988.

As a kid, Jane lived in the same neighborhood as the Dennis
boys. I knew little of their early years and asked her about life in
California. Eyes wide, her hand flew to her mouth, and she said,
"I can't talk about that!" Then fled from the room.

Mystified by her response, I forgot about it until I discovered
the obviously fictitious employment documents. Holy moly,
someone probably paid them to provide a cover story for James

and his whereabouts. "Here's your money, and you can NEVER tell anyone about this."

The O.S.S. had an unlimited and unquestioned budget to fund their work and were not above buying a story. Allied pilots captured by the Germans were universally shocked to discover their captors already knew their military history, family members, and personal interests. The spy business worked both ways; what better way to discourage curiosity than to offer up the world's dumbest employee?

There's an unanticipated consequence to the twisted record, a necessity of the time to protect an agent from evil; it continues to confuse today.

Tuesday, June 29, 1943.

BEGAN WORK AT 1230 PM. SALARY $7.12 PER DAY.

A liar, lazy, incompetent, absent without leave... give the boy a raise.

Thursday, Aug 19, 1943.

ABSENT DUE TO "COLON TROUBLE." DOCTOR NOT NECESSARY.

Another aberration. A formal record of something that 'didn't happen.'

Thursday, Sept 2, 1943.

RECEIVED MONETARY PROMOTION. $7.12 PER DAY TO $7.60 PER DAY EFFECTIVE 9/13/43.

Just in case we failed to adequately recognize his incompetence.

Tuesday, Sept 21, 1943.

DISCHARGE PENDING.

I'm sure something was ending, just not employment at the dry dock.

Thursday, Sept 30, 1943.

Last day of duty.

Left service at the Drydocks "to come home to my mother."
  Right! The same mother who is addressing her letters to him on the "U.S.S. Restorer c/o Fleet Postmaster, San Francisco, Calif." It's the C.S. Restorer, Grandma, and he hasn't been on it since January 1942.

Thursday, Oct 21, 1943.

Re-hired at Puget Sound Navy Yard in Bremerton. WAR SERVICE APPOINTMENT. HELPER-GENERAL, $7.60 PER DAY. 2ND SHIFT, RE-EMPLOYMENT.

Except, he worked at the Keyport Torpedo Station before, not PSNY.
  The deadbeat is rehired where he hadn't worked before at the highest rate he's ever earned, to do more undefined tasks. There is never a record of having learned a trade or consistently doing anything.
  Someone likes this guy.

Thursday, Oct 28, 1943.

TO BE RELEASED ON 17TH BIRTHDAY FOR ENLISTMENT IN THE NAVY.

Rehired at the Torpedo Station, he's soon up to his old tricks.
  Tricky fellow, that's one service he was never in.

Thursday, Nov 18–Sunday, Nov 21, 1943.

ABSENT FOR STOMACH FLU.

At least he's learned to spell it.

Monday, Nov 22, 1943.

PERMISSION SLIP RECEIVED FROM MOTHER WITH
CONSENT TO TAKE APPRENTICE COURSE.

*For what? Unlike every other work record I've looked at, his is strangely
silent on this point.*

Tuesday, Nov 30, 1943.

SICK LEAVE.

Oh, thank God, another day off.

Wednesday, Dec 1, 1943.

INJURY OCCURRED AT ALLIED TRADES IN THE
FOLLOWING MANNER: WORKING ON THE BACK OF THE
GARBAGE TRUCK. STEPED ON A NAIL COVERED BY
PAPER. CAUSE OF INJURY: ACCIDENITAL. NAME OF
WITNESSES TO INJURY: MICKEY O'BRIEN. SIGNED,
JAMES H. DENNIS.

DIAGNOSIS IN BRIEF: WOUNDED, PUNCTURED RIGHT
FOOT. ACTIONS TAKEN: TIRED. SENT HOME. SIGNED,
D.J. LAUER, LIEUT COMDR. (MC) U.S. NAVY.

*Really? A machinist risked a run-in with the union garbage guys? I don't
think so, but there's an even better story here.*

The injury claim form that is signed James H. Dennis but isn't
his signature is witnessed by a fellow employee, Mickey O'Brien.
Mickey may have been a fellow agent trainee who, like so many,

washed out of the program and was sent to the real army. Mickey's obituary said, "Mike served in WWII from 1942 -1944 in the Army Air Force and flew missions in Africa and Europe where he was wounded and received the Purple Heart medal."

Interesting. I wonder how he was pitching garbage into a truck at the Torpedo Station on December 1, 1943, halfway through his service with the Army Air Corps?

The Torpedo Station figures so prominently in this fiction, we decided to dig deeper into the records and noticed the person who most frequently signed 'worker trainee' Jimmy's paperwork was Tipton D. Westfall, the Torpedo Station's commanding officer.

Really? The commanding officer had nothing better to do? I hope they developed torpedoes better than they doctored documents.

Thursday, Dec 2, 1943.

SICK LEAVE.

Not again. James is no wimp. Six feet tall and about 235 pounds depending on whose paperwork you're reading. Whoever created this record had no imagination.

Monday, Dec 6, 1943.

James' 17th birthday.

Finally, old enough to join the service with his mother's permission.

Sunday, Dec 12, 1943.

ABSENT FROM WORK WITHOUT PERMISSION FOR 2 HOURS.

Again.

Thursday, Dec 16–Monday, Dec 20, 1943.

ABSENT FROM WORK DUE TO FLU. BECAME ILL AT
HOME. DID NOT SEE A DOCTOR. ABSENCE APPROVED.

Not once is he ever seriously called to task for his dismal work record. In fact, it's difficult to determine what it was he was supposed to be doing, and in spite of multiple recommendations to never rehire him, he is rewarded with a string of new jobs and pay raises.

Wednesday, Dec 29, 1943.

REQUESTED RESIGNATION TO JOIN THE U.S. ARMY
TRANSPORT SERVICE. OKAY TO RELEASE. PERMISSION
SLIP RECEIVED FROM MOTHER TO QUIT THE KEYPORT
NAVAL T. STATION TO JOIN THE ATS.

Back to the ATS? I don't think so.
  Why he needed Mother's permission "To quit the Keyport Naval T. Station," is uncertain and unnecessary because, according to the record, at this time he's employed at the Navy Yard in Bremerton.

Thursday, Dec 30, 1943.

RELEASED FOR DUTY ONLY TO JOIN THE U.S. ARMY
TRANSPORT SERVICE.

For some reason, they're pretty specific about who they want to inflict him on.

January 1944.

ASSIGNED TO THE A.T.S. SHIP, SIERRA.

The only trouble with this, and most likely why his service with her was not included in the new Honorable Discharge, the Sierra isn't an A.T.S. ship. She's the U.S.S. Sierra, a destroyer tender in the U.S. Navy. One would need to join the Navy to serve on her.

He didn't.

February 1944.

ASSIGNED CS RESTORER.

Again? Familiar with the ship, I'm sure it made sense to reassign James to her... only one problem, the gun log says she's far from land, mending cable in the Bering Sea when he is both assigned to and relieved from this short stint back in the A.T.S. Stranger yet, it appears he steps off the ship and onto dry land at Fort Knox, Kentucky, headquarters of the A.T.S.

Neat trick.

May 12, 1944.

ASSIGNED TO USAT ROSEBANK.

This ship is leased by the A.T.S., at least the one not operated by the Germans, and although the records say he was on it, he wasn't. He'd already disappeared from the face of the earth.

June 2, 1944.

Ethel mails her "Where's my son?" letter.

She's led to believe he's still on the Restorer.

September 1944.

ASSIGNED TO F-49. CREWMAN.

The record says he was on his way to the South Pacific as a crewman aboard a fictitious ship with no name and not a hint of a record, the F-49.

More good news for James; he's to receive a 100% raise in pay for "War Hazard Duty."

Oct 1944–Feb 1945.

Well-traveled, James is back at work in the Puget Sound Navy Yard where, on his work application under, 'Previous Employ-ment,' someone, not James, wrote, "Various oceangoing vessels."

Unlike every other mariner who ever served on a ship, James can't remember which ships he was on. There's a reason... he was never on those ships, and not at the Navy Yard either.

25.

Feb–Dec 1945

POST–WAR ARMY/AIR FORCE

Feb 5, 1945.

INDUCTED INTO AUS. REPORT OF PHYSICAL
EXAMINATION AND INDUCTION. FT. LEWIS WA. BROWN
HAIR, BROWN EYES. MEDICAL EXAMINER P. P. COOLEY,
MAJ. MC

Even though the fighting in Europe had ended, the enthusiasm for maintaining James' employment façade continued. Dr. P.P. Cooley, I'm sure a pleasant enough gentleman but apparently nearsighted, must have guessed at the eye and hair color. James looks like a classic Aryan with sky blue eyes and very blond hair.

What the heck is the AUS? A visit with our expert, Erik, cleared the fog. The Army, when it's in the continental U.S., is the Regular Army. Because the war was a conflict fought by many nationalities and allied armies, the Army in the field is the Army of the United States. The only way to be "inducted" into the AUS is to be standing on foreign soil, and consistent with Dad's story.

The Battle of the Bulge began with a surprise German offensive on December 16, 1944, and ended in an allied victory on January 25, 1945.

According to my father, he was repatriated in Belgium after the Battle of the Bulge.

During the battle, the Germans had sent out squads of men who'd misled convoys and conducted several successful ambushes while dressed in the uniforms of captured Americans. Germans posing as Americans were very unpopular. When caught, they were lined up and dispatched immediately. Unsure of who was whom, paranoia ran rife, and even generals were asked for their identity papers at the point of a gun.

I'm guessing here, but I wouldn't be surprised if a blond, blue-eyed, six-foot German-speaking civilian who walked into your camp without papers were immediately put in custody until his story could be checked out. Ten days, probably unpleasant ones spent in a makeshift stockade, passed between the end of the Battle of the Bulge and his "induction."

If you think the end of the war would mark a return to a normal existence and recordkeeping, you'd be wrong. The government wasn't quite finished with this former mariner, spy, and finally, a member of the armed forces. They had one or two, actually three more uses for his unique skills and experience, so the records of 1945 through most of 1948 are as indecipherable as the previous three years.

Mar 1, 1945.

NAVY DEPT, PUGET SOUND NAVY YARD. SEPARATION DUE TO INDUCTION INTO ARMED FORCES FOR WAR SERVICE. RALPH WALDO CHRISTIE, REAR ADMIRAL, U.S.N. COMMANDANT

If you insist, we'll contribute one of our worst employees to the cause. Are you kidding me–Ralph Waldo Christie, Rear Admiral, Commandant of one of the biggest navy repair facilities on the west coast, signs the paperwork of a kid, a deadbeat employee who's being drafted, but was

inducted into the AUS a month ago? You guys need to get your stories straight.

Mar 2, 1945.

ORDERED TO REPORT TO RECEPTION CENTER, FORT LEWIS, WA ON THIS DATE

He would if he could, but he's in Germany hunting bad guys.

Mar 5, 1945.

Induction document signed by James H. Dennis and witnessed by A. Peshek, Commanding Officer and Eugene L. Quirk, 1st Lieut, AUS

Real enough, A. Peshek, and Eugene L. Quirk may have witnessed a document being signed by someone, just not James. We know this because, again, it's not his handwriting.

Mar 9, 1945.

FORT LEWIS RECEPTION CENTER TO INF RTC CAMP HOOD, TEXAS. THIS SOLDIER WAS TRANSFERRED TO YOUR COMMAND PER PAR 19 SO 60D ON 9 MAR 1945 AND LEFT THIS ORGANIZATION 10 MAR 1945. HIS CHARACTER IS NOT OBSERVED. EFFICIENCY RATING AS A SOLDIER NOT OBSERVED. I HAVE PERSONALLY VERIFIED ALL ENTRIES IN THIS INDORSEMENT. M. C. SCHANANDORE, WAC, ASST. ADJ., RECEPTION CENTER, FT. LEWIS WA

Apparently, a ghost is being transferred from Ft. Lewis in Tacoma, Washington to Camp Hood, Texas. You have to give Ms. Schanandore credit, she didn't lie when she said, "I have personally verified all entries in this endorsement." Character NOT OBSERVED, efficiency rating as a soldier NOT OBSERVED.

June 20, 1945.

HEADQUARTERS IRTC CAMP HOOD, TEXAS. THIS
SOLDIER WAS TRANSFERRED TO YOUR COMMAND PER HQ
IRTC ON _____ AND LEFT THIS ORGANIZATION
_____. HIS CHARACTER IS _____.
EFFICIENCY RATING AS A SOLDIER _____. I
HAVE PERSONALLY VERIFIED ALL ENTRIES IN THIS
INDORSEMENT. CONSTANCE R. CRANE, 1ST LT., WAC,
HQ IRTC, CAMP HOOD, TX.

This is a good one. It appears Constance was a capable clerical specialist in charge of transferring invisible soldiers. The ghost arrived at Camp Hood, and now after 17 weeks of training for, well, they never say, is being sent to (not specified), and lacks character and efficiency.

July 23, 1945.

AT MADIGAN GENERAL HOSPITAL FOR HEAD INJURY

There's no supporting documentation to explain the how of the injury, and why it couldn't be handled by the local hospital. Madigan General Hospital is over two thousand miles away.

July 31, 1945.

STATION HOSPITAL, CAMP HOOD, TX. TONSILLAR
REMNANT REMOVED. LINE OF DUTY INJURY. DATE OF
ADMISSION JULY 31, 1945; DISCHARGED BACK TO
GENERAL DUTY AUG 5, 1945. ROBERT W. GILMORE,
1ST LT, MAC.

Meanwhile, back at the camp. Eight days after he was at Madigan Hospital, he's admitted to the base hospital at Camp Hood? How?

A line of duty injury, a tonsillectomy? What duty? Who's kidding who? Salt would have been added to the wound if anyone had checked his medical records. Jimmy had his tonsils removed when he was a kid.

Aug 27, 1945.

IRTC CAMP HOOD TX TO CG AGF REPL. DEPOT #4, CAMP ADAIR, OREG. THIS SOLDIER WAS TRANSFERRED TO YOUR COMMAND PER PAR 10 SO 210 AND LEFT THIS ORGANIZATION 1 SEPT 1945. HIS CHARACTER IS EXCELLENT. EFFICIENCY RATING AS A SOLDIER EXCELLENT. I HAVE PERSONALLY VERIFIED ALL ENTRIES IN THIS INDORSEMENT. FRIEDA R. KLUNDT, 2ND LIEUT. WAC, ASS'T PERSONNEL OFFICER, HQ IRTC CAMP HOOD, TEXAS.

Well, finally, whatever line of duty he was involved in rehabilitated the ghost; character is EXCELLENT, efficiency also EXCELLENT. Now he's off to Camp Adair to do what? Camp Adair, formerly a huge training center, by 1944 had been reduced to a single purpose, a prisoner of war camp for German soldiers.

So far the only person to witness James' character and efficiency as a soldier is Frieda E. Klundt who hailed from Walla Walla, WA, where we lived when I was in high school.

Oregon's Second Largest City

At a time when the population of Corvallis was only 14,000 people, as many as 30,000 to 50,000 soldiers and civilian employees lived and worked in nearby Camp Adair. Camp Adair became Oregon's second-largest city; only Portland was larger.... In July 1944, the local newspaper reported that Camp Adair had been abandoned and the soldiers sent away. When the divisions left, the U.S. Army turned the hospital at Adair over to the U.S. Navy. The Navy brought wounded men from the Pacific Theater to Adair for treatment. The hospital was enlarged to take care of about 3,600 patients.... Shortly after the last division left, part of Camp Adair served as a prisoner-of-war (POW) camp for Italians and Germans. Civilians in Benton and Polk counties were mostly unaware of the prisoners' presence. (Source: web, bentoncountymuseum.org)

Sept 5-17, 1945.

FURLOUGH.

As long as you're there, why not take a couple of weeks and kick back?

Oct 8, 1945.

HQ AGF RD#4 CAMP ADAIR OREG TO CO: PRESIDIO OF
MONTEREY, CALIF. THIS SOLDIER WAS TRANSFERRED
TO YOUR COMMAND PER PAR 5 SO 98 THIS HQ AND LEFT
THIS ORGANIZATION 8 OCT 1945. HIS CHARACTER IS
UNKNOWN. EFFICIENCY RATING AS A SOLDIER
UNKNOWN. I HAVE PERSONALLY VERIFIED ALL
ENTRIES IN THIS INDORSEMENT. JAMES O. DEVANEY,
JR., 1ST LIEUT., SIG. C, ASST. S-1, AGFRC#4.

*Back to his old status, the invisible soldier, James O. Devaney Jr. put him
on a bus for The Presidio of Monterey, headquarters of General DeWitt's
4th Army. .*

Oct 16, 1945.

HQ AGFRD #4 CAMP ADAIR, OREG. TO CO AGF RD #2
FORT ORD, CALIF. THIS SOLDIER WAS TRANSFERRED
TO YOUR COMMAND PER PAR 15 SO 106 ON THIS HQ AND
LEFT THIS ORGANIZATION 16 OCT 1945. HIS
CHARACTER IS UNKNOWN. EFFICIENCY RATING AS A
SOLDIER UNKNOWN. I HAVE PERSONALLY VERIFIED
ALL ENTRIES IN THIS INDORSEMENT. JAMES O.
DEVANEY, JR. 1ST LIEUT., SIG. C, ASST. S-1,
AGFRC#4.

*Back at Camp Adair? There's no record of the ghost being transferred
back to Camp Adair before being reassigned to Fort Ord.*

Oct 19, 1945.

ARRIVED AT FT. ORD.

Five days to get to Ft. Ord, one hundred and eighteen miles! The ghost is losing his touch.

Oct 30, 1945.

PHYSICAL EXAMINATION PRIOR TO DISCHARGE, FT. ORD, CA. EXAMINER HARRY D. GROSSMAN, CAPT, M.C.

I have no record of this exam. More invisible records for the invisible soldier.

Nov 1, 1945.

HONORABLY DISCHARGED TO REENLIST IN THE REGULAR ARMY. ENLISTMENT RECORD SIGNED BY RECRUITING OFFICER J.A. REGAN, MAJOR, AUS AGF RD#2. HQ AGF RD#2 FORT ORD, CALIF TO CO RC FORT LEWIS, WASH. THIS SOLDIER WAS TRANSFERRED TO YOUR COMMAND PER PAR 1 SO 305 ON THIS HQ AND LEFT THIS ORGANIZATION 2 NOV 1945. HIS CHARACTER IS EXCELLENT. EFFICIENCY RATING AS A SOLDIER EXCELLENT. I HAVE PERSONALLY VERIFIED ALL ENTRIES IN THIS INDORSEMENT. BOYD A. RUEGSEGGER, CAPTAIN, AGD, ASS'T ADJ. GENERAL AGF RD#2.

You can almost hear the indignant, "What the hell is this guy doing in the AUS?"

Nov 2, 1945.

ACCEPTED FOR SERVICE AT FORT ORD, CA. ENLISTED AT FORT ORD, CA ON THE 2 DAY OF NOV 1945 IN GRADE OF PFC FOR AIR CORPS TO SERVE THREE YEARS.

HAROLD C. DOWELL, 1ST LIEUT. CAC. PRIOR SERVICE,
AUS, UNASSIGNED REGIMENT, ARM, OR SERVICE, FROM
2 MAR 1945 TO 1 NOV 1945. DISCHARGED AS PVT,
CHARACTER UNKNOWN.

*Enlisted as a Private First Class is a step up from his lowly status as a
private. Now that I think about it, what's a Private doing gallivanting
around the country, anyway, and why, even though Captain Ruegsegger
endorsed his character as EXCELLENT, did 1st Lieut. Dowell once
again have no idea what his character is like? It's a mystery.*

Good questions that began to bug me. Many of the camps,
forts, and military facilities he visited were training bases, and
the rest existed for diverse purposes. I wondered, might there be
something common to them all? A question I'd never thought to
ask, and one I suspect no one else thought anyone might ask. It
took some digging, and the answer, an emphatic, yes. All were also
prisoner-of-war camps for Germans.

It was time to repatriate the captured Germans, and the U.S.
government sent men who knew Nazi officers on sight to search
through the ranks of prisoners for criminals.

Surprised shopkeepers had a good reason to be fearful of James;
his visit to their store was the second time he surprised them.

At the end of the war, they looked forward to a trip back to the
Fatherland until...

Oh Scheiße, der Donut-Junge! (Oh shit, the Doughnut Boy!)
Fingered by an eyewitness, they could be pretty sure real prison,
as compared to a POW camp, would be their most likely new
home. Sure enough, the doughnut boy arrested them then moved
on to the next camp to repeat the process.

Unbeknownst to James, the men he arrested had a trump card.
Their comrades back home, familiar with the new enemy, the Russians, were having their records whitewashed and being hired to
fill the ranks of the new C.I.A. Recognizing the American people would have little stomach for the twist in fate if they knew, to
guarantee silence, the agency gave the prisoners new names and

records, a bank account full of money, a small business, and a home somewhere in America.

Nov 5-Dec 3, 1945.

FURLOUGH. PAID FURLOUGH TRAVEL ALLOWANCE $52.45.

Discharge from the AUS and enlistment into the Regular Army apparently comes with a perk. A month of FURLOUGH. Okay, I'll accept the month off for reenlistment, but I wonder at the travel allowance, and where was he between the end of the furlough and his transfer to Greensboro on December 23, hanging around Fort Ord for twenty days?

Dec 23, 1945.

AAF BU GREENSBORO NC TO: AQ-B125-RR-A(A). THIS SOLDIER WAS TRANSFERRED TO YOUR COMMAND PER PAR 71 SO 355 ON THIS HQ AND LEFT THIS ORGANIZATION 23 DEC 1945. HIS CHARACTER IS UNKNOWN. EFFICIENCY RATING AS A SOLDIER UNKNOWN. I HAVE PERSONALLY VERIFIED ALL ENTRIES IN THIS INDORSEMENT. E.M. KERNEN, 1ST LIEUT., A.C.

The ghost is back to his old tricks; apparently, once again, no one has seen this soldier who has no job and receives no training.

Dec 30, 1945.

ENTERED FOREIGN SERVICE, NEW YORK PORT OF EMBARKATION, ENTRY IN SERVICE RECORD.

At least he has a service record now although it's pretty sketchy about details.

26.

1946

The record suggests nothing about how he got there or why he was sent, although he did. "I was at The Nuremberg trial because I had arrested a number of people who were to be tried."

Jan 8, 1946.

ARRIVED IN GERMANY

Jan 15, 1946.

TOOTH FILLED AT DENTIST, NUREMBERG.

No question about it, in spite of documented claims that he was 'never overseas,' the dentist in Nuremberg repaired a filling.

Jan 25, 1946.

ETO INDOCTRINATION COURSE.

I'd guess everyone who served in Germany sat through this.

Feb 6, 1946.

SERVED IN GER. 6 FEB 1946.

That stamp on his service record makes it official, by February 6th he was someplace in Germany.

Feb 15, 1946.

CASUAL POOL AAF/ET REINFORCEMENT DEPOT
(PROV) FURSTENFELDBRUCK, GERMANY APO 208 (PROV),
TO: CO HQ & BASE SERV. SQ. 42ND AIR DEPOT ANSBACH
GERMANY. THIS SOLDIER WAS TRANSFERRED TO YOUR
COMMAND PER PAR 4A SO 46 AND LEFT THIS
ORGANIZATION 18 FEB 1946. HIS CHARACTER IS
UNKNOWN. EFFICIENCY RATING AS A SOLDIER
UNKNOWN. I HAVE PERSONALLY VERIFIED ALL
ENTRIES IN THIS INDORSEMENT. HAROLD H. WOOD,
WOJG USA HQ & HQ CO 70TH RD

Of all places the ghost might have been sent, an air repair depot seems unlikely, considering he's received no training for the activity. To make the point, while at Ansbach, he has no work record.

Ansbach, home of the 42nd Air Depot is only a thirty-minute train ride from Nuremberg and apparently is 'home away from home' for the men involved with the trial.

The following information from website www.billmuster.com, was written by his daughter, Nori Muster.

Nuremberg Trials
Photos by Bill Muster

My father took the Nuremberg Trial photos when he was a twenty year old sergeant and aircrew member in the U.S. Army Air Force. Military records confirm that he did basic training in Las Vegas April 2-June 23, 1945, joined the Army in Seattle November 15, 1945 (five days before the start of the trial), departed for Germany February 3, 1946, and then returned to America December 7, 1946 (two months after the Nuremberg Trial ended). He was discharged from the Army several weeks later, February 11, 1947.

While living in Germany, he was stationed in Ansbach, a short train ride to the west of Nuremberg. He was a publicist, section head, and photo chief for the base. Besides photographing the Nuremberg Trials, he took photos for the Ansbach Record, a weekly paper for American GIs in Germany. In his discharge papers, under "summary of military occupations," it says: PHOTOGRAPHIC CHIEF: SERVED WITH THE 42ND AIR DEPOT FOR TEN MONTHS. PERFORMED THE DUTIES OF A PHOTOGRAPHER WHILE ENGAGED IN WORKING WITH INTELLIGENCE AND OPERATIONS. DID A GREAT DEAL OF AERIAL AND GROUND WORK IN CONNECTION WITH MAKING TOPOGRAPHICAL MAPS. ALSO ASSISTED IN KEEPING A CHECK ON LINES OF SUPPLY. PREPARED AND MIXED SOLUTIONS, DEVELOPED FILMS, AND RETOUCHED NEGATIVES. ALSO DID A VARIETY OF INDOOR JOBS SUCH AS PORTRAITS AND PHOTOSTATS. SUPERVISED THE WORK OF 9 MEN AND LAB PERSONNEL. SERVED 10 1/2 MONTHS IN THE EUROPEAN THEATER OF OPERATIONS.

At least Bill had a job during his truncated military career. He grew up in Chicago but was supposed to have been inducted in, of all places, the same as Dad who wasn't there, Seattle, and then sent to photograph the first trial of its kind, at the end of which he's immediately discharged. Two stripes on his shoulder, he was made Photographic Chief of the 42nd Air Depot and got a third stripe, then worked with intelligence and operations, and engaged in aerial survey work? Who are they kidding? Someone wanted Bill for the job.

Oh yeah, he worked in the darkroom, doctored photos, and was pressed into service taking glamour shots.

As I write about it, I wonder if Bill was behind the camera that took the only picture of my father in a uniform, a uniform strangely devoid of all emblems of rank or accomplishment on a soldier who totally lacked military bearing.

Aerial survey work? Bill's work record is the only document I've seen that mentions aerial work, although Dad told a story about killing time hunting the small German deer from the back of an airplane. In one of his letters he wrote his mother about an attack of colitis while flying over Germany. Who knows?

Both Bill and Dad went through Greensboro at the same time.

Will wonders never cease.

Seems Bill was able to enlist as a Corporal. He must have been something special with his high school education, no prior military experience, and "Skilled occupations in the production of bakery products" to earn the rank of Corporal upon enlisting. Nowhere in the bio he wrote is a mention of him making bakery products, but it's right there on his enlistment record from the National Archives.

Also, Bill's mother and grandparents were as German as they come. Try "Moldenhauer" on for size, "an ancient German surname". Both his grandparents were born in Brumberg, Germany.

Right there is the likely connection. Photography is only a pastime for Bill, but he probably speaks (or at least understands) German like a local, he was raised by his German grandparents, and who would you rather have in the room with a bunch of Nazi criminals than a German-speaking photographer?

William Newton Muster (Bill) moved to Los Angeles in 1953 and died there in 1989.

In 1986, Bill was diagnosed with terminal mesothelioma due to exposure to asbestos as a painter's helper refurbishing ships for WWII at the Bremerton shipyards in 1944.

Oh no, not the Bremerton Navy Yard again.

In spite of Bill's record, enlistment in Greensboro, NC, his family has documents that suggest he went to basic training in Nevada then enlisted in the Army Air Corps.

Once again, this investigation suggests something is fishy here.

The sequence is wrong; one enlists then goes to basic training although in this case that's difficult because there was never a basic training camp in Nevada.

According to his own bio, he arrived at Bremerton sometime in 1944 and graduated from high school that June. Maybe he worked at the navy yard over the summer. Or, maybe he didn't work at the navy yard at all, like some other people we know.

He enlisted at Greensboro 13 days before Dad arrived there. Another record says he enlisted in Seattle. They just can't make up their minds.

At any rate, now he has the Navy Yard, Greensboro, Germany, the rank of sergeant (*how did he become a sergeant in less than two months? Someone likes Bill, too*) the 42nd Air Depot, Nuremberg, supply lines, orphan/abandonment, same age, interest in photography, and bakery products in common with Dad.

There's a good chance they knew each other.

Name:	William N Muster
Birth Year:	1926
Race:	White, citizen (White)
Nativity State or Country:	Indiana
State of Residence:	Illinois
County or City:	Cook
Enlistment Date:	15 Nov 1945
Enlistment State:	North Carolina
Enlistment City:	Greensboro
Branch:	No branch assignment
Branch Code:	No branch assignment
Grade:	Corporal
Grade Code:	Corporal
Term of Enlistment:	One year enlistment
Component:	Regular Army (including Officers, Nurses, Warrant Officers, and Enlisted Men)
Source:	Enlisted Man, Philippine Scout or recall to AD of an enlisted man who had been ——————— transferred to the ERC ———————
Education:	4 years of high school
Civil Occupation:	Skilled occupations in production of bakery products, n.e.c.
Marital Status:	Single, without dependents
Height:	00
Weight:	006

What, another ghost? The National Archive record lacks his height and weight.

56. *Students wore an OSS-issue fatigue uniform or "sterile" Army khakis without rank or insignia." Unlike his friend on his right, The Doughnut Boy's uniform is devoid of all insignia.*

Feb 25, 1946.

HQ & BASE SV SQ. 42AD. TO: CO 42 AIR REP SC. THIS
SOLDIER WAS TRANSFERRED TO YOUR COMMAND PER
PAR 11 SO 47 LEFT THIS ORGANIZATION 25 FEB 1946.
HIS CHARACTER IS UNKNOWN. EFFICIENCY RATING AS
A SOLDIER UNKNOWN. I HAVE PERSONALLY VERIFIED
ALL ENTRIES IN THIS INDORSEMENT. TOBIN
ARMSTRONG 1ST LIEUT. A.C.

*1st Lieut. TOBIN ARMSTRONG, who crash-landed his P-51 at Ans-
bach a few days before James arrived there, processes the ghost into the
repair depot.*

As long as we're analyzing unusual events, Mr. Armstrong is as
good a subject as any other. He may or may not have anything to
do with James and his strange story, but the coincidence of their
intersection makes his story worth a short diversion. What follows is a truncated version of his obituary.

Tobin Armstrong, 82, a Texas rancher with strong political ties,
served for nearly half a century as director of a leading cattle industry association. For forty-eight years he directed the Texas and
Southwestern Cattle Raisers Assn., a lobby and law enforcement
group.

A onetime Kenedy County commissioner, Armstrong owned the
50,000-acre Armstrong Ranch near Kingsville in south Texas. His
wife, Anne, is the former U.S. ambassador to Britain and advisor to
presidents Nixon and Ford, and just about every prominent Republican regarded an invitation to the ranch necessary, and tacit
endorsement.

The couple regularly played host at the ranch to President George
W. Bush, Vice President Dick Cheney and former President George
H.W. Bush. Another prominent guest, Prince Charles, once played
polo on the Armstrongs' lawn.

Armstrong's grandfather was a Texas Ranger who became famous
for capturing the notorious outlaw John Wesley Hardin and is
thought to have purchased the ranch with the bounty.

Possibly influenced by the lieutenant, James became a lifelong Republican, and fell in love with the North American P-51 Mustang.

Feb 26, 1946.

RECEIVED RATING: PRIVATE FIRST CLASS, PRINCIPAL DUTY: FIRE FIGHTER.

Well, finally, assigned to some kind of specific training, things are looking up.

May 31, 1946.

BEGAN FIREFIGHTER TRAINING.

Three, long boring months later? Time filled with what?

Aug 1, 1946.

PROMOTED TO CORPORAL, FIRE FIGHTER

Only ten months in the Regular Army, excellent student, so capable, let's call him a firefighter and give him a promotion.

Sept 1, 1946.

FIRE FIGHTER TRAINING COMPLETE

What a guy, all that good news back in August, a promotion and rating as a firefighter came a month before the end of the training.

Sept 1946.

INJURED WHILE ON DUTY IN BRUCK OPERATING AN AIR HAMMER WHICH BROKE.

This one is especially interesting. Injured on duty in Bruck in September 1946 (we don't know the exact date, says the Army. Really?) when an 'air hammer' exploded is not just unlikely, it was impossible because he wasn't transferred there until October 5, 1946.

Oh yeah, one more thing, air hammers, better known as rivet guns, don't blow up or otherwise present a threat when they fail, they just quit functioning, and I should know. I've been an aircraft mechanic, among other things, for five decades.

Possibly more to the point, according to the report, a 'piece of metal' hit him in the back and shattered his clavicle. When did the Army ever describe a projectile in such an obscure manner?

Oct 4, 1946.

FROM: 42 AIR REP SQ ANSBACH AIR DEPOT. TO: CO 5TH AIR VEHICLE REPAIR SQ BRUCK GER. THIS SOLDIER WAS TRANSFERRED TO YOUR COMMAND PER PAR 2 SO 134, HQS AAD AND LEFT THIS ORGANIZATION 5 OCT 1946. HIS CHARACTER IS EXCELLENT. EFFICIENCY RATING AS A SOLDIER EXCELLENT. I HAVE PERSONALLY VERIFIED ALL ENTRIES IN THIS INDORSEMENT. ROBERT P. CARUSO, CWO USA, ASS'T PERSONNEL OFFICER.

Finally, transferred to the Air Vehicle Repair Squadron at Bruck, and miracle of miracles, as Bob Caruso attests, and in spite of having done nothing for nine months, is an Excellent soldier with an Excellent character.

All right, let's look at the calendar. The ghost arrived in Germany on January 8th, six weeks after the Nuremberg trial began which seems like a long time, but this trial will become the longest in history, ten months and ten days. It ended on October 1, 1946, and four days later, curiously, the ghost is transferred from Ansbach to Bruck.

Magically, his character is excellent, and rating as a soldier is also Excellent, although as yet, he's received no training as a soldier unless you count his time in basic training, which, according to his service record, he received on the boat while in transit to Germany.

The report of an injury at Bruck in September is an obvious fabrication as he isn't transferred to Bruck until October 4. This single discrepancy impeaches all the preceding mumbo jumbo.

Dad told me, "I was at the Nuremberg trial because I arrested a number of high ranking Nazis and would need to testify. A total waste of time; a farce meant to make the world think we really took care of the bad guys. They all failed to appear."

If it looks like a duck, walks like a duck, and quacks like a duck, it's probably a duck. Just as he said, he was there.

I suppose I should have figured it out sooner, but, as the record writers intended when they created the fragmented and indecipherable documents, I fell for the lie, got lost in the attempt to make sense of the twisted tale and completely missed it. There's more than one story going on here.

Just a coincidence? Assigned to Ansbach for the vast majority of the trial, no job, no work record, and only thirty-five miles away from Nuremburg, his presence there is not the only mystery. One plus one, equals four.

What Happened to the Bad Guys?

I'll spare you my attempt to explain the unexplainable and simply offer this, an example of Winston Churchill's insight.

"The enemy of my enemy, is my friend."

What follows is a direct quote from the writer, Pulitzer Prize-winning investigative journalist Eric Lichtblau.

In Cold War, U.S. Spy Agencies Used 1,000 Nazis
By Eric Lichtblau
OCT. 26, 2014
WASHINGTON — In the decades after World War II, the C.I.A. and other United States agencies employed at least a thousand Nazis

as Cold War spies and informants and, as recently as the 1990s, concealed the government's ties to some still living in America, newly disclosed records and interviews show.

At the height of the Cold War in the 1950s, law enforcement and intelligence leaders like J. Edgar Hoover at the F.B.I and Allen Dulles at the C.I.A. aggressively recruited onetime Nazis of all ranks as secret, anti-Soviet "assets," declassified records show. They believed the ex-Nazis' intelligence value against the Russians outweighed what one official called "moral lapses" in their service to the Third Reich.

The agency hired one former SS officer as a spy in the 1950s, for instance, even after concluding he was probably guilty of "minor war crimes."

And in 1994, a lawyer with the C.I.A. pressured prosecutors to drop an investigation into an ex-spy outside Boston implicated in the Nazis' massacre of tens of thousands of Jews in Lithuania, according to a government official.

Evidence of the government's links to Nazi spies began emerging publicly in the 1970s. But thousands of records from declassified files, Freedom of Information Act requests and other sources, together with interviews with scores of current and former government officials, show that the government's recruitment of Nazis ran far deeper than previously known and that officials sought to conceal those ties for at least a half-century after the war.

In 1980, F.B.I. officials refused to tell even the Justice Department's own Nazi hunters what they knew about 16 suspected Nazis living in the United States.

The bureau balked at a request from prosecutors for internal records on the Nazi suspects, memos show, because the 16 men had all worked as F.B.I. informants, providing leads on Communist "sympathizers." Five of the men were still active informants.

Refusing to turn over the records, a bureau official in a memo stressed the need for "protecting the confidentiality of such sources of information to the fullest possible extent."

Some spies for the United States had worked at the highest levels for the Nazis.

One SS officer, Otto von Bolschwing, was a mentor and top aide to Adolf Eichmann, architect of the "Final Solution," and wrote policy papers on how to terrorize Jews.

Yet after the war, the C.I.A. not only hired him as a spy in Europe, but relocated him and his family to New York City in 1954, records show. The move was seen as a "a reward for his loyal postwar service and in view of the innocuousness of his [Nazi] party activities," the agency wrote.

His son, Gus von Bolschwing, who learned many years later of his father's ties to the Nazis, sees the relationship between the spy agency and his father as one of mutual convenience forged by the Cold War.

"They used him, and he used them," Gus von Bolschwing, now 75, said in an interview. "It shouldn't have happened. He never should have been admitted to the United States. It wasn't consistent with our values as a country."

When Israeli agents captured Eichmann in Argentina in 1960, Otto von Bolschwing went to the C.I.A. for help because he worried they might come after him, memos show.

Agency officials were worried as well that Mr. von Bolschwing might be named as Eichmann's "collaborator and fellow conspirator and that the resulting publicity may prove embarrassing to the U.S." a C.I.A. official wrote.

After two agents met with Mr. von Bolschwing in 1961, the agency assured him it would not disclose his ties to Eichmann, records show. He lived freely for another 20 years before prosecutors discovered his wartime role and prosecuted him. He agreed to give up his citizenship in 1981, dying months later.

In all, the American military, the C.I.A., the F.B.I. and other agencies used at least 1,000 ex-Nazis and collaborators as spies and informants after the war, according to Richard Breitman, a Holocaust scholar at American University who was on a government-appointed team that declassified war-crime records.

The full tally of Nazis-turned-spies is probably much higher, said Norman Goda, a University of Florida historian on the declassification team, but many records remain classified even today, making a complete count impossible.

"U.S. agencies directly or indirectly hired numerous ex-Nazi police officials and East European collaborators who were manifestly guilty of war crimes," he said. "Information was readily available that these were compromised men."

None of the spies are known to be alive today.

The wide use of Nazi spies grew out of a Cold War mentality shared by two titans of intelligence in the 1950s: Mr. Hoover, the longtime F.B.I. director, and Mr. Dulles, the C.I.A. director.

Mr. Dulles believed "moderate" Nazis might "be useful" to America, records show. Mr. Hoover, for his part, personally approved some ex-Nazis as informants and dismissed accusations of their wartime atrocities as Soviet propaganda.

In 1968, Mr. Hoover authorized the F.B.I. to wiretap a left-wing journalist who wrote critical stories about Nazis in America, internal records show. Mr. Hoover declared the journalist, Charles Allen, a potential threat to national security.

John Fox, the bureau's chief historian, said: "In hindsight, it is clear that Hoover, and by extension the F.B.I., was shortsighted in dismissing evidence of ties between recent German and East European immigrants and Nazi war crimes. It should be remembered, though, that this was at the peak of Cold War tensions."

The C.I.A. declined to comment for this article.

The Nazi spies performed a range of tasks for American agencies in the 1950s and 1960s, from the hazardous to the trivial, the documents show.

In Maryland, Army officials trained several Nazi officers in paramilitary warfare for a possible invasion of Russia. In Connecticut, the C.I.A. used an ex-Nazi guard to study Soviet-bloc postage stamps for hidden meanings.

In Virginia, a top adviser to Hitler gave classified briefings on

Soviet affairs. And in Germany, SS officers infiltrated Russian-controlled zones, laying surveillance cables and monitoring trains.

But many Nazi spies proved inept or worse, declassified security reviews show. Some were deemed habitual liars, confidence men or embezzlers, and a few even turned out to be Soviet double agents, the records show.

Mr. Breitman said the morality of recruiting ex-Nazis was rarely considered. "This all stemmed from a kind of panic, a fear that the Communists were terribly powerful and we had so few assets," he said.

Efforts to conceal those ties spanned decades.

When the Justice Department was preparing in 1994 to prosecute a senior Nazi collaborator in Boston named Aleksandras Lileikis, the C.I.A. tried to intervene.

The agency's own files linked Mr. Lileikis to the machine-gun massacres of 60,000 Jews in Lithuania. He worked "under the control of the Gestapo during the war," his C.I.A. file noted, and "was possibly connected with the shooting of Jews in Vilna."

Even so, the agency hired him in 1952 as a spy in East Germany — paying him $1,700 a year, plus two cartons of cigarettes a month — and cleared the way for him to immigrate to America four years later, records show.

Mr. Lileikis lived quietly for nearly 40 years, until prosecutors discovered his Nazi past and prepared to seek his deportation in 1994.

When C.I.A. officials learned of the plans, a lawyer there called Eli Rosenbaum at the Justice Department's Nazi-hunting unit and told him "you can't file this case," Mr. Rosenbaum said in an interview. The agency did not want to risk divulging classified records about its ex-spy, he said.

Mr. Rosenbaum said he and the C.I.A. reached an understanding: If the agency was forced to turn over objectionable records, prosecutors would drop the case first. (That did not happen, and Mr. Lileikis was ultimately deported.)

The C.I.A. also hid what it knew of Mr. Lileikis's past from lawmakers.

In a classified memo to the House Intelligence Committee in 1995, the agency acknowledged using him as a spy but made no mention of the records linking him to mass murders. "There is no evidence," the C.I.A. wrote, "that this Agency was aware of his wartime activities."

This article is adapted from "The Nazis Next Door: How America Became a Safe Haven for Hitler's Men," by Eric Lichtblau, published by Houghton Mifflin Harcourt.

A version of this article appears in print on October 27, 2014, on Page A1 of the New York edition with the headline: In Cold War, U.S. Spy Agencies Used 1,000 Nazis.

Oct 4, 1946.

TRANSFERRED TO BRUCK.

The record is strangely silent for the next five months.

27.

1947

Mar 1, 1947.

RECEIVED RATING: SERGEANT.

Only fourteen months in service, and although there's no record he turned a screw or set a single rivet, they'd like to give him another promotion.

Apr 26, 1947.

QUALIFIED TO RENDER HAND SALUTE.

The nearest thing to a military education he'd ever receive unless you count basic training on the boat, and the training to be a fireman at a base that has no use for another firefighter.

May 2-11, 1947.

FURLOUGH.

Yet another vacation from the rigors of... ?

May 12–June 2, 1947.

Undocumented.
Still no grease on his hands.

June 3–13, 1947.

FURLOUGH.

The boredom is inhuman, we better give him some time off from...?

June 14–July 15, 1947.

Undocumented.
Yawn...

July 16–Aug 22, 1947.

BRUCK AIR ORDNANCE DEPOT, 3077 EUROPEAN AIR
MATERIEL COMMAND.

*Eleven months of duty at Bruck so undistinguished the Army keeps no
records, not even financial records which in the past have been so important that James' $2.30 laundry bills were tracked.*

They may not have a story to fill this time, but I do, the one he
told me, and so bizarre it must be true.
You can't make this stuff up.

Self-Employment

Remember back when James was supposed to have sailed into
harm's way on a ship that didn't exist and received a 100% increase
in pay for 'War Hazard Duty'? He also assigned half his pay to his
mother. Half of double is equal to a regular paycheck and consistent with one of Grandma's proudest stories. "When he was in
the Army, your Dad sent me his whole paycheck."
Grandma told me the story, so it must be true because, good

news or bad, Grandma had no mercy for childish feelings and didn't pull her punches or lie.

After months sitting around waiting to testify against Nazis who would never appear, the trial ends, and four days later James is quickly transferred from Ansbach to (who ever heard of it) Bruck in the mountains of Bavaria.

At yet another Air Repair Station, the question is, what do they do with an untrained airman?

"The commanding officer frowned when he read my service record. 'It says here you're a fireman. I need someone to run the fire brigade, you want the job?'

"It sounded more interesting than peeling potatoes, and that's where I was destined, so I neglected to explain the difference between a maritime fireman who made fire and a fireman, who put it out.

"'Yes, Sir,' I answered with no idea how to run a fire brigade.

"'Fine, the firehouse is on the far side of the base; you'll have to hire a crew. Use these requisition forms to order supplies. We commandeered some fire equipment from the firehouse in town. You'll need to find someone who knows how to operate it.'"

Sure enough, a historical website for the Bruck Fire Brigade has this to say: "In 1945 the Allied forces confiscated the whole equipment except one old fire engine. Hans A. Remele took over command on May 9, 1945. He and his men were confronted with a nearly empty depot."

When Dad told me that story, he made no mention of previous training. The records created retroactively that suggest he was trained as a firefighter are an embellishment, an attempt to legitimize the position. Inducted as a buck private February 5, 1945, the dumbest employee in the history of the Navy Yard is a private first class nine months later, and a corporal in eighteen months. A soldier of unknown efficiency and character, it doesn't seem like he should qualify as an 'Exceptional Performer,' a distinction required to be promoted to sergeant in less than three years. Instead, he's promoted March 1, 1947, after two years and one month. As always, the Ghost gets whatever he needs, a rank consistent with his new responsibilities as airbase fire chief.

"I knew I was in over my head, so I went to town and found an experienced firefighter, Fritz, to be my adjutant. Fritz ran the day-to-day operation, and I did the paperwork."

I accepted his story at face value until one day, years later, a question occurred to me. "I understand why you had your check sent to Grandma during the war, but how'd you get along without cash afterward?"

Slow to respond, he thought about it and surprised me with an answer so short it could only be the truth.

"I didn't need any money; I had plenty."

"You didn't need any money," I stupidly repeated.

"Nope."

"You had plenty?"

"Yup."

Not so easily brushed off as I was as a child, I employed my rapier-like wit and probed on.

"How?"

He looked at me over his reading glasses, sighed, and must have understood; I wasn't gonna quit.

"Well, hell, the fire station was on the far side of the base, miles from the rest of the facilities, and a little world of its own. If we did our job, no one ever came to check on us. I was allowed supplies for twenty men and one day while I was typing up the supply requisition forms for the week, a thought occurred to me. If, after typing the 'two' key, I hit the 'zero' key twice instead of once, ten trucks would arrive with supplies instead one. If anyone complained, I could always claim it was a typo."

"What happened?"

"The next week, ten trucks arrived. We unloaded them and had to take a fire engine outside to make room for the stuff."

"Did anyone complain?"

"No, things were pretty confused at the time."

It should have been obvious, but I just had to ask.

"What did you do with all the extra stuff?"

"Operated the black market in Bruck. The locals came to the firehouse to buy food and medicine that still wasn't available in town. My costs were low; so were my prices. I was very popular."

If I ignore the activity of the records and just look at the places and dates, his letters and stories and Grandma's are the only part of the records I have that hold water.

Aug 15, 1947.

ORDERS TO TRANSFER TO CAMP KILMER, NJ. (FROM) 5TH AIR VEH. DEPOT APO 66 U.S. ARMY TO: TDY W/PARA CM, CAMP KILMER NJ. THIS SOLDIER WAS TRANSFERRED TO TDY-YOUR COMMAND PER P8 SO 77 HW EUROPEAN AIR MATERIEL COMMAND AND LEFT THIS ORGANIZATION 15 AUG 1947. HIS CHARACTER IS EXCELLENT. EFFICIENCY RATING AS A SOLDIER EXCELLENT. I HAVE PERSONALLY VERIFIED ALL ENTRIES IN THIS INDORSEMENT. ROBERT C. HEATH, 1ST LIEUT. A.C.

Uh, oh, this looks like the end of the gravy train for a soldier doing his job with excellence. James had added ambition to his early opportunistic self-employment, planned to stay in Germany, attend the University of Heidelberg, and expand a new relationship with a young woman.

For some reason I couldn't fathom, he's not transferred immediately, but instead is once again furloughed for a month.

Aug 23–Sept 21, 1947.

FURLOUGH. STRUCK BY A PIECE OF METAL IN LEFT ARM MID-SEPT. INJURY DID NOT REQUIRE HOSPITALIZATION.

What the heck, another 'piece of metal,' and a government form to report that nothing happened. Who does that? Not the U.S. Army for sure.

Maybe no hospitalization in Bruck, but just wait, the machine will get into high gear in a minute.

The report plays down the severity of the event. A hand grenade landed on the roadway behind James and a friend as they walked home from a night on the town.

Bang! The shrapnel from the grenade was not chunks of steel from a U.S. grenade, but thousands of tiny slivers unique to a German grenade designed to maim rather than kill. A wounded soldier required several more to care for him.

As a kid, I assumed the attack was the result of a disgruntled local, but dissecting these records leads me to believe there might have been a different motive, a darker one. Bruck is a small town; James has provided a source of much-needed food and medicine. He isn't the guy you ambush.

"Are you afraid of Germans?"

"No, I'm afraid of Americans..."

57. Welcome to Camp Kilmer

Sept 15, 1947.

DEPARTED GERMANY WHILE ON FURLOUGH. STRUCK BY
A PIECE OF METAL IN MID-SEPTEMBER.

The 15th is pretty close to "mid-September."

Sept 16, 1947.

ARRIVED IN U.S.

One day later, a very junior airman is back in America, and not
just back, but supposedly temporarily assigned to Camp Kilmer
with no job or job history while he was there. Maybe no employment, but the camp did have exactly what James needed, a one-
thousand-bed hospital for injured soldiers returning from
Europe.

There was the answer to the question, why transfer him to
Camp Kilmer then give him a furlough?

They didn't.

For some reason, they didn't want him in the hospital in Bruck,
so had 1st Lieutenant Robert Heath backdate a transfer to the
largest war wound recovery hospital in the U.S. where he arrived
the next day. The only way to do that is to fly, and that's exactly
what he told me happened.

"The day after I was fragged, they flew me to a hospital in the
states. I left my stuff in the terminal except for the antique beer
stein which I took into the restroom with me. When I came back,
everything was gone."

*The stein was in our home until Dad died and now is on a shelf at my
brother Jim's place.*

Oct 14, 1947.

PAE WESTOVER FIELD
MASS TO: 314TH BU MCCHORD FIELD, WASH. THIS

SOLDIER WAS TRANSFERRED TO YOUR COMMAND
PER 9ND SO 77 1ST IND EUROPEAN AIR MATERIEL
COMMAND, COMO APO60 AND LEFT THIS ORGANIZATION
18 AUG 1947. HIS CHARACTER IS UNKNOWN.
EFFICIENCY RATING AS A SOLDIER UNKNOWN. I HAVE
PERSONALLY VERIFIED ALL ENTRIES IN THIS
INDORSEMENT. M. J. LEEN, CWO U.S.A ADJ.

Stationed at Westover Field, Camp Kilmer New Jersey for a month; once again he's had no job and has turned back into the ghost of unknown character and efficiency.

Nov 17, 1947.

HQ 414TH AFBU MCCHORD FIELD WA TO: CO 62ND
TROOP CAR WG. MCCHORD FIELD WA. THIS SOLDIER
WAS TRANSFERRED TO YOUR COMMAND PER PAR
8 SO 169 HQ AND LEFT THIS ORGANIZATION
17 NOV 1947. HIS CHARACTER IS UNKNOWN.
EFFICIENCY RATING AS A SOLDIER UNKNOWN. I HAVE
PERSONALLY VERIFIED ALL ENTRIES IN THIS
INDORSEMENT. PAUL D. ALLEN, 1ST LIEUT. A.C.

Headquarters transfers the ghost to a local troop carrier wing who have no use for him.

58. Dad's beer stein

28.

1948

Feb 18-27, 1948.

IN HOSPITAL FOR SURGERY TO REMOVE SHRAPNEL FROM LEFT ARM.

Oh, no longer a 'piece of metal', now it's a piece of shrapnel. Conveniently adjacent to Mc Chord Field is the largest military hospital in the northwest, Madigan General Hospital where James spent nine days.

March 3, 1948.

ADMITTED TO MADIGAN GENERAL HOSPITAL DUE TO CAR ACCIDENT.

A masterpiece of understatement; in a car accident three days after his last visit to the hospital, he's probably still wearing his armband.

In 2016, we called the local police department to see if they could offer any insight into this accident. The young man who answered the phone, obviously looking at a computer screen, proceeded to read the 1948 accident report while we frantically transcribed his words. He cited the information down to the last detail. When he finished, I asked, "Can you send me a transcript of that?"

"No, I'm sorry, we don't keep records that old!" he exclaimed, and abruptly hung up.

Months spent spying on the German high command, and now we're supposed to believe my father is the most unlucky sergeant in the Air Force.

After the trial, disillusioned when his testimony wasn't required at Nuremberg because the men he arrested didn't show up, he's transferred to Bruck, where his luck turns for the worse.

He's hit in the back by a 'piece of metal' with enough force to take out his clavicle, supposedly a fragment of a tool in front of him that can't explode.

Let's call it what it probably was. Shot in the back.

Next, he's unsuccessfully ambushed with a grenade by persons unknown.

But not likely locals.

Then with no broken fingers, arms or legs, injuries common to car accidents, he's hospitalized for six months in a body cast with injuries supposedly sustained in a car wreck on a quiet residential street. A wreck that totaled the car and threw James, asleep on the back seat a half hour after they left the base, seventy-five feet. The driver escaped without a scratch, the front seat passenger disappeared, and the 'totaled' car was returned intact to its owner a few days later.

Someone drugged him and tried to kick him to death.

Insult added to injury, in the military hospital, he's pumped full of drugs whose known side effect is memory loss.

Someone didn't like James, or rather, was uncomfortable with what he knew, and when they couldn't kill him, tried to wipe out his memory.

"No, I'm not afraid of Germans, I'm afraid of Americans."

Viola probably said it best when she wrote to the Army on his behest.

What follows is an unedited transcript of her handwritten letter.

Veterans Adm
Seattle WA

Dear Sir-

In regards to questions, reverse of this paper pertaining to injuries and illness incurred by my son, Sgt. James H. Dennis, during his time (I believe 4 years) in Service U.S. Army. To my knowledge, my Son hasn't been the same since he came home from Germany, as he had numerous carbuncles on neck and attack of colonitis (colon) after passing out in plane over Germany (In Air Corp). On his return home I hardly recognized him, but most serious effects I noticed were from injuries received from car accidents, after his return home. As near as I can remember he was hospitalized at Ft Lewis Madigan General Hosp. for 7-8 months before discharge. From severe head injuries about eye and forehead that part of his head is still numb, also eyesight very bad, also bad scars on face (eye & forehead) He has severe headaches taking aspirin in A.B.C constantly. He had severe shoulder arm and chest (broken ribs) injuries, in cast long periods of time, It was necessary to remove bone (part) from left shoulder. His left arm is allmost useless, so far as manual labor is conscerned, and his shoulder allmost constantly pains him, also while at Madigan complications caused some type of severe illness causing extremely high temperature and was in isolation ward. It was some type of lung congestion possibly caused from broken ribs. Also after his discharge from hospital (before he married) he was home with me and I noticed he was continually on the stool, bowels either loose, or constipated. I don't know if this condition still exists. He is moody and at times sullen, whereas before he was happy & cheerful; being the Mother of 3 disabled Sons (veterans) one totally, I know something of the suffering and trouble these men have in an effort to live a normal life and earn a living.

Signed,
Viola Olson

PO Box 595
Keyport Wash

March 4–Sept 3, 1948.

IN HOSPITAL. MAY 1–(FROM) SQ. C,
62ND ADRM. GP. MCCHORD AFB, WA TO: CO, DET OF PAT.
MAD. GEN HOSP. THIS SOLDIER WAS TRANSFERRED TO
YOUR COMMAND PER HTO# 277. HIS CHARACTER IS
EXCELLENT. EFFICIENCY RATING AS A SOLDIER
EXCELLENT. I HAVE PERSONALLY VERIFIED ALL
ENTRIES IN THIS INDORSEMENT. ORDEAN T. OLSON,
1ST. LT. USAF, ADJ. SO C.

Once again, the ghost is revealed for what he truly is, a well-traveled enlisted man with no training, no work experience, EXCELLENT character, and EXCELLENT efficiency.

What a guy!

Aug 10, 1948.

COMPLETED HIGH SCHOOL GED AFTER 27 WEEKS OF
STUDY.

While in a body cast, in Madigan Hospital... good job, James. Oh, wait a minute, March 4th to August 10th is only twenty-two weeks, sooo... GED school began January 28th. Give or take a day, long before he entered the hospital on March 3rd. November 17, 1947, he was transferred to the 62nd TROOP CAR Wg. MCCHORD FIELD WA.

I suppose he could have squeezed in the twenty-seven weeks of school around shrapnel removal surgery, a car wreck/mugging, and six months in the hospital.

I apologize if I sound paranoid, but who wouldn't be after this snipe hunt? James is plenty smart; with only an eighth-grade education and a GED, he graduated from Western Washington University in three years.

Sept 3, 1948.

DOP, MADISON GH, TACOMA WASH TO: SQ C, 62ND ADRM
GP, MCCHORD AFB, WASH. THIS SOLDIER WAS
TRANSFERRED TO YOUR COMMAND PER PAR 5
SO#199 AND LEFT THIS ORGANIZATION 2 SEPT 1948.
HIS CHARACTER IS UNKNOWN. EFFICIENCY RATING AS
A SOLDIER UNKNOWN. I HAVE PERSONALLY VERIFIED
ALL ENTRIES IN THIS INDORSEMENT. CLYDE W.
GRUNWALD, WOJG USA MIL PERS OFFICER.

The record says he was transferred to the Administration Group
as a typist. There's no record he was ever trained to do anything,
let alone be a typist.

The new career was doomed.

He never learned to type in the classic fashion, but after years of
practice, he could type like a machine gun with only two fingers.

October 1948.

ISSUED LAPEL BUTTON FOR NO LOST TIME.

*Who are they kidding, over what period of time? He was just discharged
from a six-month stay in the hospital on September 3rd.*

October 7, 1948.

DISCHARGED FROM ACTIVE DUTY FOR CONVENIENCE OF
GOVERNMENT (NOT FOR REASONS OF PHYSICAL
DISABILITY).

*Can't kill him, can't train him, no good for nothing, we hope he can't
remember his name, get rid of him.*

Are they serious?

PART V

IN THE END...WAS THE BEGINNING

29.

A New Leaf

There are no work records from the time, only a vague reference to having worked in the shipyard in October 1948. For sure he married my mother, Joyce Young, Jinx to her friends, in the Lutheran Church across the street from her home in Poulsbo on November 19, 1948. By September 1949, he was enrolled at Western Washington University at Bellingham, and on October 1, 1949, I complicated their lives.

I'd never known my mother had a nickname until it was revealed in a high school yearbook. Jinx? Not anything like her character, it must have been a reference to something or someone in popular culture of the day.

It didn't take long to figure it out.

Jinx Falkenburg. The world's first 'Super Model.'

Mother was a looker.

I'm not sure how he accomplished it, but three years later, June 1948, Dad graduated with a degree in special education.

We moved to Everett, WA, July 5, 1952, where he took a job teaching kids with special needs until we moved to Portland in June 1953 at the end of the school year. Note: in 1952, 'Special Needs' children had speech and/or hearing difficulties. Children with learning disabilities were lumped under the category of 'retarded' and placed in state-operated institutions.

59. Mom and Dad's wedding photo

60. Jinx Falkenburg

OUT OF THE ROAR OF BATTLE COMES SMOOTHER HEARING

Here is a graphic sample of what Sonotone means by "watching over your hearing" instead of just handing you a hearing aid and saying, "God bless you".

Two years ago the U.S. Signal Corps gave Sonotone the job of making radio headsets for the fighting forces. It was a tough job. The new headset had to be cut down in size to fit under the Army's new battle helmet. It had to work under any climatic conditions from a New Guinea jungle to a Kiska fog. And it had to give *sure-fire* hearing under battle conditions from the roar inside a tank or the confusion of a beach head, all the way to a break-through barrage.

Skipping details... half a million of those hard-to-make headsets are making history with America's fighting men... and incidentally, along with other war work, have won for Sonotone the award of the coveted Army and Navy "E". But (*and this will interest every hard of hearing person in America!*) ... in working with the Signal Corps Technical Staff on this radio headset, Sonotone engineers developed a new principle of frequency control to make hearing astonishingly easier and smoother. *Today* that easier and smoother hearing is yours!

Mind you, we said *today.* This is no post-war promise. Utilizing this new principle of frequency control, Sonotone has designed a new series of air conduction receivers. They enable the Consultant to fit a Sonotone much more exactly to your hearing loss. They give you *strain-free* hearing... smoother... easier... much less tiring over a long day. They eliminate nervous tension. And today, at this very minute, they are waiting for you in Sonotone offices all over the country.

As you perhaps have read in our advertising, Sonotone is devoted to the one idea of trying to give you BETTER HEARING. We have no interest in just selling you a hearing aid. The Sonotone Consultant knows it is his duty to measure your hearing loss, to fit a Sonotone to your *personal* needs, to teach you how you use your Sonotone most effectively, and day or night to be at the other end of your telephone to make sure that your hearing never fails you. The promptness with which this new war-born development is now made available to you is just another example of how Sonotone constantly watches over your hearing... AND WHY IT PAYS TO WEAR A SONOTONE.

REACH THE TOP WITH SONOTONE

Many men from highly paid professions have found a richer life and a new security as Sonotone Consultants. More men of ability and character are always needed, for the number of Sonotone users is steadily increasing. New Consultants find confidence in the rigorous technical training which enables them to give the best scientific analysis and correction of hearing losses available today. They find strength in the fact that Sonotone research laboratories, the largest devoted exclusively to hearing aids, have the longest and most imposing record of hearing aid improvements. Above all, they gain pride and a respected place in their communities and lifetime security by carrying out the Sonotone Creed that has brought such growing hosts of people BETTER HEARING! For details visit your nearest Sonotone office, or write King Cooper, Vice President, Sonotone Corporation, Elmsford, N.Y.

SONOTONE *A personal service that seeks to give you* BETTER HEARING *FOR THE REST OF YOUR LIFE. Accepted by the Council on Physical Medicine of the American Medical Association.*

There are over 155 Sonotone offices. The office nearest you is listed in your local telephone directory. Phone for information or write SONOTONE, ELMSFORD, N.Y. *In Canada: write 229 Yonge St. Toronto. In England, 144 Wigmore St., London, W. 1. Also available in the world's principal countries.* If you live in the U.S.A. write for a free copy of "Hearing Through the Years". © 1944, Sonotone Corp.

Out of nowhere, a new industry magically appeared at the end of the war, technology made possible by two things.

The first, research contracted out by the Army Signal Corps for the benefit of the O.S.S., America's first clandestine service, produced hearing aids that were just that, secret gadgets to give allied soldiers 'super hearing,' able to detect enemy activity far beyond the normal audible range.

The second, America's enthusiasm for out-producing the enemy had filled warehouses with surplus equipment. As the war wound down, the question arose, what to do with the unused inventory? How to dispose of Jeeps, light planes, rifles, ammunition, boots, uniforms, and the like was obvious, the ubiquitous Army Surplus Store, but what do you do with secret technology to enhance hearing?

The answer, clever repurposing, and a new opportunity for men from inside the clandestine service who knew about secret gadgets, men who became hearing aid salesmen. No fool, James climbed on the bandwagon and went to work in Portland as man-

ager at R.J. Marion Company, a distributor of Radioear and Audi-
vox brand hearing aids.

In January 1955, James bought the Audiphone business in the
Hollywood district and renamed it Hollywood Speech and Hearing Clinic.

61. Me in Dad's car

At the new office, he set up a workbench for me where most
Saturdays I sat on a tall stool and built plastic model airplanes
while he worked with clients who couldn't come to the office during the week.

Saturday mornings I could be found by myself, window shopping outside of Vic's Hobby Shop while I waited for them to
open. I had a dollar and twenty-five cents in my pocket. Ninety-
eight cents for the model, twenty-five cents to purchase a pack of
Camel cigarettes for Dad at the corner grocery, and two cents for
me to buy two pieces of black licorice.

I liked the office where, when I was done building the model, I spent time in the small soundproof booth, wore the headsets that hung on a hook under the window, and pretended I was Flash Gordon on a space adventure.

Every couple of months, Dad and I went on a journey, a trip to see clients too infirm to travel from their homes in central Oregon. He loaded a suitcase into his 1937 Chevrolet, and I climbed on his lap from where I did most of the driving. Well, the steering part. On the road, we ate at hamburger stands, stayed in motels with a swimming pool, and generally had a fine time.

Invited into their homes, I watched while he patiently and respectfully fit hearing aids and taught people with severe hearing loss to speak. A clever teacher, he avoided what might have been an awkward process.

"Let's call your tongue Mr. Wellington; your mouth is his home. Sometimes he goes upstairs, sometimes down, or wherever necessary to form words." His clients loved him for his delicate and dignified treatment of their condition. I watched him and learned to respect and defend anyone with a disability, a lesson that would lead to my one and only assault on another human.

Unintended Consequences

"Okay, you kids just hop up in the back of the truck. It's only a half-hour ride to the pool."

Without a pool of our own, summer camp meant two times a week, thirty of us rode in a covered two-ton truck for an afternoon of play in the pool of a local resort. We sat fifteen in a row on the floor of either side and faced each other. My good friend Brian sat directly across from me where I happened to sit next to a deaf girl I didn't know, Linda.

I don't remember who said what, but Linda responded in the high-pitched, flat monotone of someone who has never heard a human voice. Brian made a mistake when he made fun of her, and a circuit breaker of indignation in my head popped. Mindless, I flew across the truck, landed on Brian with my hands around his throat, and screamed, "You can't make fun of her like that!"

Out of my mind, I think I fully intended to choke him to death as half a dozen friends pulled me off. The incident terminated with the two of us making up, but neither quite sure what had happened.

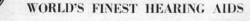
62. Dad's ad in the 1956 Portland City Directory

30.

One Last Encounter
with Normal

On his beloved island of Maui, Dad had one last encounter with an aging Nazi.

While having lunch with my youngest brother at the Intercontinental Hotel, something caught his eye mid-bite. "Don't turn around. There's a family birthday party happening on the other side of the room. It's the old man's birthday. He's here with his children and grandchildren. I'm certain he's been living in South America."

A few minutes passed.

"Dang, the General's wife has spotted me. Be cool; she's gonna come over here."

The old lady left the party, walked to the lobby, down a short corridor that led to a door on Dad's side of the room, then walked along the windows that looked out on the sea.

She stopped behind his chair, her back to his, and gazed out the window. A quiet conversation in German lasted a few minutes until she left the way she had come.

Wide-eyed, my brother asked, "What did you talk about?"

"She begged me not to arrest him, said it was his birthday. He has cancer, and those are his children and grandchildren. I told her not to worry, enjoy the party; she had nothing to fear from me."

Do What You Love

He loved to fish. June 24, 1977, pleased as punch, he caught his last fish, a barracuda.

He also loved to free dive in the ocean around his home on Maui, Hawaii. He was in the best condition of his life, and his collection of rare Maui spindles proved it. The mollusk is only found below sixty feet, and his younger friends hated diving with him.

Years later, in a conversation with Mother, she said, "You know, don't you, he lied to us about life after a heart bypass. He knew he had about three years to live before the bypasses clogged up. He told me he was never going back to the hospital. Normally when he went diving, he slipped silently from the house, but he woke me and said goodbye before his last dive."

Two weeks after his visit at our house, June 25, 1977, he died of a heart attack while diving for spindles at Makena Landing.

63. Dad, June 24, 1977, the day before he died.

31.

In the End... was the Beginning

Strangers in the uniform of Hawaii, flower shirts, shorts and flip-flops, rode across the bay huddled together in an ugly, shapeless fiberglass box on a catamaran hull, their awkward silence enforced by a howling outboard.

With ten fathoms of water under her hull, the hideous, carnival-orange blob lay quietly, surrounded by a blue cloud of exhaust and shimmering oil slick on a luminous blue sea under a postcard-perfect Hawaiian sky.

Self-conscious in my flip-flops and shorts purchased for the occasion, a desperate attempt to fit into the one-dimensional season, I knelt on the deck while someone spoke soothing words about a man he hardly knew.

Trained early by stoic Scandinavians, "We don't show it, no tears," was our 'normal' way to cope with indescribable loss, but in my heart, black as midnight, a cauldron of pain seethed, furious I was forced to share my grief with strangers. Breath, strangled by unalloyed bands of pain, came in shallow gulps.

The little box is heavier than I expected.

Always calculating, he discovered the VA would pay all the

expenses for cremation and left instructions to do so. He'd figured out how to leave life with little more than a ripple.

On my knees, kneeling over the edge of the boat, muscles deprived of oxygen, I fumbled with the twisty thing around the neck of the plastic bag.

Eyes, useless as a pair of grapes, unexpectedly filled with tears and added their salt to the ocean.

Mental seams unraveled, tightly bound self-control failed, and the protective cloak of fabricated dignity slid from my shoulders.

Oh, God no!

Damn!

Quit whining. Go ahead, tip the box.

I'd been involuntarily holding my breath, anoxic, incapable of coordinated motion, but inevitably forced to suck air, my lizard brain sorted the uncertain horizon and rediscovered down.

There ya go, now just don't fall in.

With a hiss, gravity, reliable as ever, drew the grey-white, surprisingly chunky ash into the sea when I finally upended the cardboard container.

Mesmerized, I watched a mottled grey slick of dust form on the surface as the cascade of human sand fell gracefully through sixty feet of crystal ocean, struck the bottom, and bloomed into an emerald green flower.

Look at that, a silent, inverted green mushroom cloud, counterpoint to the fiery fingerprint of a ruptured hydrogen atom.

While my father's ashes silently slid into oblivion an ear-splitting scream, trapped in my head, longed to escape.

Death, surprise enough, was amplified by his choice of interment in the sea. These strangers, his new friends, believed the choice to be emotionally symbolic, a love for Makena Landing, favorite place to dive, how and where he died. 'A heart attack, complicated by drowning,' said the death certificate

One more way a man of elaborate secrets who I dearly loved, but really never knew, holds affection at arm's length and guarantees no one will grieve quietly beside a stone marker.

Old at thirty-five, convinced he would never see forty, death caught up at fifty, and now I felt ancient at twenty-seven.

My seven-year-old, the same age as me when my beloved grandmother died, felt the loss as intensely as anyone and quietly sobbed by herself in the corner.

Before the scream in my head could escape, the dark spell was broken by the vibrations of vaguely religious music from someone's guitar. The strangers joined in song, cast their flower leis into the sea and created an unintentional multicolored base for the inverted mushroom cloud.

Wrapped in their own grief, preoccupied with song, they allowed me, known only as "Jim's oldest," safe in anonymity, to fade from the group to comfort my child and choke down this most bitter pill.

Someday, I'm going to figure out who you really were.

64. The boat from which I released Dad's ashes

Or, Maybe Not

Shortly before he passed, our father sent this to Jim, his namesake and today, a fellow pastor.

Jim,

Dietrich Bonhoeffer was born February 4, 1906. Who was Dietrich Bonhoeffer? Was he a spy? a martyr? a theologian? a musician? a genius? a pastor? This list could keep going, but would never end. Not even Bonhoeffer could answer the question of who he was. This is a poem which he wrote, I pray that it helps you understand Bonhoeffer, and yourself, to a fuller extent.

Dad

I think Dad meant, "understand me".

"WHO AM I?"

Who am I? They often tell me
I stepped from my cell's confinement
calmly, cheerfully, firmly,
like a Squire from his country-house.
Who am I? They often tell me
I used to speak to my warders
freely and friendly and clearly,
as though it were mine to command.
Who am I? They also tell me
I bore the days of misfortune
equally, smilingly, proudly,
like one accustomed to win.
Am I then really all that which other men tell of?
Or am I only what I myself know of myself?

Restless and longing and sick, like a bird in a cage,
struggling for breath, as though hands were
compressing my throat,
yearning for colors, for flowers, for the voices of birds,
thirsting for words of kindness, for neighborliness,
tossing in expectation of great events,
powerlessly trembling for friends at an infinite distance,
weary and empty at praying, at thinking, at making,
faint, and ready to say farewell to it all?
Who am I? This or the other?
Am I one person to-day and to-morrow another?
Am I both at once? A hypocrite before others,
and before myself a contemptibly woebegone weakling?
Or is something within me still like a beaten army,
fleeing in disorder from victory already achieved?
Who am I? They mock me, these lonely questions of mine.
Whoever I am, Thou knowest, o God, I am thine.

-Dietrich Bonhoeffer

"Success is not final, failure is not fatal - It is the courage to continue that counts."

Winston Churchill

65. *The Dennis Family, Haines, Oregon 1963*

Timeline

The timeline is a potpourri of records received from numerous disassociated sources that, by and large, are a fabrication. His official military records are still locked under a presidential seal, along with the Nuremberg records, until 2045. Our aim was to tease the truth out of the hodgepodge of documents, letters, and stories.

ACTIVITY	Start Date	End Date
James Henley Dennis born to Clarence Ray & Viola Ethel Dennis.	Dec 6, 1926	
Clarence passed away, died on USS New Orleans.	Sept 3, 1941	
Job – Porter, Black Ball Ferry Station, Seattle WA.	Oct 1941	Dec 1941
15th Birthday	Dec 6, 1941	
Job – CS Restorer, setting pins in a bowling alley at Bamfield Cable Station during attack on Pearl Harbor.	Dec 7, 1941	
CS Restorer ordered to Seattle for Wartime Service., Crew conscripted into Army Transport Service duty.	Dec 8, 1941	
USAT Restorer left Victoria, BC and sailed to Seattle on orders from the army.	Dec 19, 1941	
Voyage to unknown destination aboard unknown vessel (assume CS Restorer).	Dec 20, 1941	Jan 7, 1942
No documentation during this time period.	Jan 9, 1942	Nov 11, 1942
Formation of OSS.	Sept 1942	
Viola Ethel Dennis married Oscar Olson.	Nov 12, 1942	
16th Birthday	Dec 6, 1942	
Mechanic learner at Naval Torpedo Station, Keyport, WA. Ethel wrote permission for James to be an apprentice.	Dec 11,1942	
Mention in Kitsap County Herald that James entered service in March 1943.	Mar 1943	
Working at Puget Sound Navy Yard.	Jun 1943	
Requested resignation to "go tuna fishing". Request denied.	Jun 8, 1943	
Separation granted.	Jun 18, 1943	
US Naval Drydocks, Terminal Island CA. "Helper".	Jun 29, 1943	

Last day of duty. Left to "come home to my mother".	Sept 30, 1943	
Rehired at Puget Sound Navy Yard, Bremerton, WA.	Oct 21, 1943	
17th Birthday	Dec 6, 1943	
Released from torpedo station duty "only to join the Army Transport Service". Ethel wrote permission for James to join the ATS.	Dec 30, 1943	
Signed oath at Embarkation Headquarters that he wasn't working for another government agency.	Dec 31, 1943	
Assigned to USA Training ship "Sierra" as a wiper.	Jan 3, 1944	Jan 20, 1944
Promoted from wiper to fireman on Sierra.	Jan 21, 1944	Feb 4, 1944
Designated mother as beneficiary on war risk benefits.	Feb 7, 1944	
Transferred to CS Restorer as a wiper, Promoted to fireman on April 21, 1944.	Feb 6, 1944	May 11, 1944
Transferred to USAT Rosebank as an oiler. June 2, Ethel sends a letter wondering where he is. Note: Rosebank was under German control for the duration of the war. His discharge papers state he was on the Rosebank from May 12 – Sept 3.	May 12, 1944	Aug 15, 1944
On Leave.	Aug 16, 1944	Sept 3, 1944
Transferred to F-49 vessel in the Southwest Pacific area of operations. Oiler. 100% pay increase due to war hazards.	Sept 4, 1944	Nov 3, 1944
Recommended for separation. "You refuse to continue your present employment because of the discharge of the Master and 1st Assistant Engineer and you are not desirous of shipping out with any other Master and 1st Assistant Engineer."	Nov 3, 1944	
Working as a machinist helper at Puget Sound Navy Yard, according to what James wrote on a later employment application.	Oct 1944	Feb 1945

Discharged from F-49 vessel at Fort Knox, KY.	Nov 13, 1944	
18th Birthday. Battle of the Bulge begins Dec 16, 1944.	Dec 6, 1944	
Inducted into General Military Service, Army of the US, Port Orchard, WA. Brown hair, brown eyes, fair posture, 224 lbs, 5'10" tall.	Feb 5, 1945	
Place of entry into service: Ft. Lewis, WA. Active duty, Army of the US.	Mar 2, 1945	Mar 9, 1945
Transferred to Camp Hood, TX. Private, Army of the US, unassigned regiment. Suffered a case of colitis sometime during 1945.	Mar 10, 1945	Jun 5, 1945
Qualified to use the MK-M1 rifle.	Apr 20, 1945	
End of WWII in Europe. James is part of 172nd Training Battalion, Company C, IRTC.	May 8, 1945	
Transferred from Camp Hood, TX to unknown location.	Jun 6, 1945	
Head injury in Madigan General Hospital, Tacoma WA.	Jul 23, 1945	
Tonsils removed, in hospital at Camp Hood, TX.	Jul 31, 1945	Aug 3, 1945
Discharged from hospital.	Aug 4, 1945	
No documentation.	Aug 5, 1945	Aug 31, 1945
Transferred to Camp Adair OR, traveled for three days.	Sept 1, 1945	
Arrived at Camp Adair.	Sept 4, 1945	
Furlough.	Sept 5, 1945	Sept 17, 1945
Transferred to the Presidio, CA.	Oct 8, 1945	Oct 15, 1945
Transferred to Fort Ord, CA.	Oct 16, 1945	Oct 30, 1945
Transferred to Fort Lewis, WA. Honorably discharged from AUS, 4th regiment, Co. D to enlist in regular army.	Nov 1, 1945	
Enlisted in regular army, Ft. Lewis WA, Private 1st Class. Assigned Air Corps – 3 years.	Nov 2, 1945	
Reenlistment furlough.	Nov 2, 1945	Dec 1, 1945

Qualified to use carbine weapon while on furlough.	Nov 10, 1945	
19th Birthday	Dec 6, 1945	
Sent to Overseas Replacement Depot (ORD), Greensboro NC, Three days' travel time.	Dec 8, 1945	Dec 11, 1945
Arrived at ORD.	Dec 12, 1945	
Began Basic Training.	Dec 17, 1945	
Transferred from ORD to unknown command.	Dec 23, 1945	
Departed for foreign service.	Dec 30, 1945	
Completed basic training en route to Germany.	Jan 1, 1946	
Arrived in Germany.	Jan 8, 1946	
Received tooth fillings in Nuremburg.	After arrival in Germany	
European Theater of Operations Indoctrination Course completed.	Jan 25, 1946	
Received orders to transfer to Ansbach Germany, 42nd squadron.	Feb 18, 1946	
Received rating, Private first class. Principal duty: Replacement.	Feb 20, 1946	
Transferred to 42nd Air Repair Squadron.	Feb 25, 1946	
Received rating: Private first class, principal duty: Fire fighter.	Feb 26, 1946	
Began Fire fighter training, received orders to wear the European, African, Middle Eastern Theater Ribbon. Later crossed out.	May 31, 1946	
Received rating: Corporal, fire fighter.	Aug 1, 1946	
Fire fighter training complete.	Sept 1, 1946	
Injured while on duty in Bruck operating an air hammer which broke. It was noted that he was not hospitalized for this injury. German grenade shrapnel?	Sept 1946	
Transferred to 5th Air Vehicle Repair Squadron in Bruck.	Oct 5, 1946	

Six and a half months with no documentation.	Oct 6, 1946	Apr 30, 1947
20th Birthday	Dec 6, 1946	
Received rating: Sergeant, 405th Air, US Army.	Mar 1, 1947	
Qualified to render hand salute.	Apr 26, 1947	
Furlough.	May 2, 1947	May 11, 1947
Undocumented.	May 12, 1947	Jun 2, 1947
Furlough.	Jun 3, 1947	Jun 13, 1947
Undocumented.	Jun 14, 1947	Jul 15, 1947
At Bruck Air Ordnance Depot, 3077 European Air Material Command.	Jul 16, 1947	Aug 22, 1947
Received orders to transfer to Camp Kilmer, NJ from headquarters of European Air Material Command.	Aug 15, 1947	
Received assignment to McChord Field, WA. Rating: Sergeant, Squadron 62C.	Aug 18, 1947	
Furlough. Struck by a piece of metal in left arm, mid-September. From what?	Aug 23, 1947	Sept 21, 1947
Departed Frankfurt Germany while on Furlough.	Sept 15, 1947	
Arrived in US.	Sept 16, 1947	
At Westover Field.	Sept 22, 1947	Nov 16, 1947
Transferred to the Department of the Air Force.	Sept 26, 1947	
Received orders to transfer to McChord Field.	Oct 14, 1947	
Undocumented.	Oct 15, 1947	Nov 16, 1947
Arrived at McChord Field, 414th Army Air Force.	Nov 17, 1947	Feb 17, 1948
21st Birthday	Dec 6, 1947	
Records altered to indicate home address change from Poulsbo WA to Norfolk VA. 62nd Airdrome Group, Squadron C.	Feb 6, 1948	
Qualified to use a carbine weapon.	Feb 13, 1948	

In McChord Hospital for surgery to remove shrapnel from left arm. Nine days in hospital.	Feb 18, 1948	Feb 27, 1948
Admitted to Madigan General Hospital due to car accident.	Mar 3, 1948	
Transferred to McChord Hospital, six months in hospital.	Mar 4, 1948	Sept 3, 1948
Records altered to indicate Ethel's change of address from Poulsbo to Norfolk.	Jun 1, 1948	
Completed high school GED after 27 weeks of study. How?	Aug 10, 1948	
Discharged from hospital back to active duty.	Sept 3, 1948	
Became a typist at McChord Field.	Sept 4, 1948	
Lapel Button issued for "No Lost Time". How?	Oct 1948	
Discharged from active duty for convenience of government (not for reasons of physical disability.) No disability – really?	Oct 7,1948	
Examination for Civil Service Commission.	Oct 10, 1948	
Began working at Puget Sound Navy Yard, according to what he wrote on a later job application.	Oct 1948	
Married Joyce Young.	Nov 19, 1948	
22nd birthday	Dec 6, 1948	
Moved to 445 High St, Apt 2, Bellingham WA. Student at Western Washington University.	Sept 1949	
Birth of first son, Michael, in Bellingham WA.	Oct 1949	
Student, WWU.	1951	
Graduated Western Washington University.	Jun 1952	
Moved to Broadmoor Apartments, Everett WA.	Jul 5, 1952	
Special Education Teacher, Everett WA school district. Birth of first daughter.	Sept 1952	Jun 1953

Moved to Portland, 4122 SE 113th Ave. Manager at RJ Marion Co. (Distributors for Radioear and Audivox hearing aids).	Jun 1953	
Purchased Audiphone Co. Lived at 12924 NE Schuyler, Portland. His brother William Dennis is also listed on a Radioear ad; they must have been working together.	Jan 1955	1956
Speech and Hearing Therapist at his company, Hollywood Speech and Hearing Clinic. 8 months at Western Conservative Baptist Seminary. Same home address.	1957	1958
Still in Portland and still owned Hollywood Speech and Hearing at 3915 NE Hancock St. Third son born April 1959	1958	1961
Moved to Haines, OR. Pastor. Haines First Baptist Church. 1961, birth of second daughter.	Sept 1961	Jun 1964
Moved to 201 N 1st St Dayton WA. Pastor, Dayton Conservative Baptist Church.	Jul 1964	May 1966
Moved to 828 N. 9th St Walla Walla WA. Prison Chaplain at Walla Walla State Penitentiary; Pastor, Bethel Baptist Church, Milton-Freewater, WA.	Jun 1966	Mar 1969
Walla Walla VA Hospital, Chaplain. Retired as VA Chaplain Jan 25, 1976 and received disability.	Apr 1, 1969	Jan 25, 1976
Moved to 515 Island Surf Condo, Kihei, HI. Prison Chaplain.	Feb 1976	
Moved to 1866 Anapa Place, Kihei, HI, last address.	Aug 1976	
Passed away while swimming.	Jun 25, 1977	

Photo Credits

Cover photo, James H. Dennis, most likely taken by Bill Muster.

1. Dad and Me at Lake Whatcom. Dennis Family Collection
2. Cessna 140. Digital image. From the Archives: Wolfgang Langewiesche Flies Across Africa. Web 5 May 2018 <https://airfactsjournal.com>
3. Grandpa and Me. Dennis Family Collection
4. Legacy. Source: Michael Dennis Private Collection
5. Stick and Paper Airplane. 2014 Chris Crowder
6. P-51 Service Manual. Digital image. NA-5865C P-51D Mustang NAA Maintenance Manual. Web 5 May 2018 <http://pioneeraerosvc.com>
7. Haines Depot. Michael Dennis Private Collection
8. Riding Mower. Digital image. Web 5 May 2018 <http://www.mytractorforum.com>
9. Haines in Winter. Michael Dennis Private Collection
10. Haines Main Street. Michael Dennis Private Collection
11. Jim, me, and Happy. Dennis Family Collection
12. Awards Day. Dennis Family Collection
13. Certificate of Merit. Dennis Family Collection
14. Family in 1963. Dennis Family Collection

15. Steve and Me Shaking Hands. Dennis Family Collection
16. Van Patten Lake. Digital Image. Web 7 May 2018. US Forest Service, public domain
17. The Lodge at Little Alps. Michael Dennis Private Collection
18. Steve and Me, fearless. Dennis Family Collection
19. Ski at Little Alps. Dennis Family Collection
20. Mike and Models. Dennis Family Collection
21. Pittman Farm. Michael Dennis Private Collection
22. Spillway. Source: Michael Dennis Private Collection
23. Spillway Graphic. US Army Corps of Engineers, public domain
24. E6B. Source: Michael Dennis Private Collection
25. Dad and Me. Dennis Family Collection
26. Mom and Me. Dennis Family Collection
27. Bruce's Candy Kitchen. Digital image. Cannon Beach History Walking Tour. Web 5 May 2018 <https://cbhistory.org>
28. Leaving Pendleton. Michael Dennis Private Collection
29. First Solo. Michael Dennis Private Collection
30. RG and Me. Michael Dennis Private Collection
31. Irv and Me. Michael Dennis Private Collection
32. Champ. Digital image. Web 5 May 2018 <http:Pin-img.com>
33. Paper Airplane. Digital image. Web 5 May 2018 <http://country929.com>
34. Perry Whiting Book Cover. Michael Dennis Private Collection
35. Camp X. Digital image. Camp X Official Site. Web 5 May 2018 <http://www.camp-x.com>
36. Dad and Me. Dennis Family Collection
37. Sprinkler Article. 17 Nov 1975 Walla Walla Union-Bulletin

38. Halfway House Article. 29 Aug 1971 Walla Walla Union-Bulletin
39. Dad in his office. Dennis Family Collection
40. Heart Association Award. Jim Dennis
41. F-89. Public domain
42. P-51 Schematic. Digital image. Web 5 May 2018
43. Bob's P-51. Michael Dennis Private Collection
44. Bob, Jude, and Mike. Michael Dennis Private Collection
45. Jude, Mike, and Alon. 1985 Michael Dennis Private Collection
46. Honorable Discharge. 2018 Michael Dennis Private Collection
47. Certificate of Release. 2018 Michael Dennis Private Collection
48. Letter. 2018 Michael Dennis Private Collection
49. Letter. 2018 Michael Dennis Private Collection
50. Victory Medal & Lapel Button. 2017 Chris Crowder
51. Letter. 2018 Michael Dennis Private Collection
52. Letter. 2018 Michael Dennis Private Collection
53. Article about Jim. 15 June 1973 Walla Walla Union-Bulletin
54. Marriage License. Michael Dennis Private Collection
55. Keyport Torpedo Station. Digital image. From Steam to Electronics 1950-59. Web 5 May 2018 <https://maritime.org>
56. Dad and Friend. Quote from an article about the OSS, *Kill or be Killed* by Patrick J. Chaisson. *"Put away were all personal possessions and clothing; instead, students wore an OSS-issue fatigue uniform or "sterile" Army khakis without rank or insignia."* Dennis Family Collection
57. Camp Kilmer. Digital image. Camp Kilmer Debar-

kees Booklet. Web 5 May 2018 <http://thewar-box.blogspot.com>

58. Beer Stein. Jim Dennis
59. Wedding photo. Dennis Family Collection
60. Jinx Falkenburg. Digital image. Web 5 May 2018 <http://david-paris.blogspot.com>
61. Radio Ear ad. Michael Dennis Private Collection
62. Me in Car. Dennis Family Collection
63. Dad and Fish. Dennis Family Collection
64. Funeral. Michael Dennis Private Collection
65. Dennis Family. Dennis Family Collection